SOLO

SOLO
Self-Portrait of an Undercover Cop

Anthony Schiano with Anthony Burton

DODD, MEAD & COMPANY
New York

58912

For the men of the New York City Police Department
and Albert Schiano

ISBN: 0–396–06856–1
Library of Congress Catalog Card Number: 73–9274
Printed in The United States of America
by The Haddon Craftsmen, Inc., Scranton, Penna.

Foreword

Perhaps only New York City could produce a cop in the extraordinary mold of Detective Anthony Schiano. In many ways, he reflects the contradictions and the diversity, the toughness and the humanity of the city. A second-generation Italian-American, he joined the police department while his school pals were settling comfortably into the highways and byways of crime. New York gave him a chance and he took it.

Some police officers go the book route, studying to achieve promotion via the examination room. These are the new breed who will bring education to bear as a weapon against villainy.

Others, like Schiano, who has only a basic education, work on the streets where the hard reality is the mugger with a knife, the pusher with a gun. It's a different sort of education in the South Bronx, in Harlem—one where failure in an examination can mean a knife in the back.

Detectives like Schiano are not heard on TV or radio because their accents are inelegant and because they cannot use the language of social workers and psychiatrists. To them, a punk is a punk, not the victim of a rapacious system.

Anthony Schiano knows this because he knows how close

he came to being a punk himself. He decided to go another direction. It wasn't that easy, but it was that simple.

Schiano doesn't look like a cop, which was one reason he survived nine years in the most dangerous duty the New York City Police Department can offer—working as an undercover narcotics detective making buys from pushers on rooftops and in alleys of the city's slums.

He doesn't look like the holder of the department's Combat Cross and God knows how many citations. He doesn't look as though he's been shot, stabbed, beaten—sometimes by fellow cops—although a closer look reveals the scar on one thumb, caused by a narcotics pusher who was trying to shoot him in the back of the head at the time.

A slim, wiry man with dark wavy hair, he looks mild enough to be a waiter or a druggist. A bank teller, maybe. The only thing that contradicts that image is the tension in his manner, particularly when he gestures Cagney-style with stiff fingers while talking.

The years in dirty old clothes sitting in crummy bars, waiting on street corners, climbing tenement stairs to meet a man who, at the very least, will be carrying a knife—they leave a residue of strain, and Schiano's nightmares sometimes wake his wife.

During those nine years of undercover work, Schiano took the name Tony Solo, because he worked alone. He preferred it that way. He preferred it, for one reason, because twice he was nearly murdered while working undercover with partners.

Instead of looking to others for help, Solo relied on his own unique combination of guts, strength, bravery, humor and startlingly unconventional weapons. Then, when he had finished his day's work, he would leave the dirty streets, the junkies, the shadowy alleys and he would drive home to become just another suburban homeowner contemplating the menace of the dandelions and crab grass on his front lawn.

Except for the knowledge that the next day he would have to return.

Solo is through with buying narcotics now, but he's still Tony Solo to the street people. He still calls himself Tony Solo. Even after eighteen years in the department, Detective Schiano is a romantic.

But his story is true—as true as the litter in the streets, as true as the junkie nodding off on West 126th Street, as true as the flashing knife on a tenement stairway. Only the names have been changed to protect the identities of men and women who continue Solo's work.

Anthony Burton

1

THE last week of August, 1971 . . . sonofabitch, it's hot in more ways than one, the weather and the number of street crimes reported to the 41st Precinct. All over the South Bronx, the rate of muggings, robberies, pocketbook snatchings and taxicab stickups is as high as the temperature.

My partner, Eddie Dillon, and me are bitching about the number of cases we're catching. We can't keep up with the case load.

This particular day, I'm in Eighth District Robbery on the second floor of the stationhouse when my boss, Lieutenant Bill Poster, comes over and says, "Hey, Tony, you hear about the policewoman who got taken off by some pushers? Over on Hoe Avenue?"

He hands me this yellow complaint form and I read that this policewoman, her name's Mary Sloan, is working undercover for the Narcotics Division when she walks into an alleyway to buy some junk and she's jumped by three guys. She gets cut, punched, and one guy sticks a gun at her head but when he tries to shoot, it misfires. Twice. She's a lucky broad. They attack her because they see her buy-money, $130, and they want it.

I'm a bit pissed off when I read this because before I came

1

to the robbery squad, I did undercover work for nine years and I knew this policewoman should never have let these punks see her buy-money. She got in trouble because she screwed up.

When I was undercover, I carried a roll of five dollar bills in one pocket. In the other, a roll of ones. If the price was $12, I'd take two fives from one roll and two ones from the other without once taking the rolls out of my pockets. That way, I didn't have to front my money.

What the hell, I'm not undercover any more. Now I'm Detective first grade Anthony Schiano, not the greasy, freaked-out Tony Solo that all the street guys, the pushers and the junkies, used to know. Me and Eddie Dillon, we're robbery detectives, so we catch this case because there's a robbery involved. There's a lot of pressure since it's a policewoman and she's been hurt.

I interview her and her back-up team who've grabbed one of the pushers who attacked her. She's a cocky kid, I think, who doesn't really know her way around. After this, she wants to get out of undercover work. That's the way with most of them . . . after a year or so, they've had enough.

Eddie Dillon and me, we go to the Hoe Avenue area and start questioning people, harassing the junkies, telling them we're going to take them in if they don't tell us who jumped the policewoman. We get lucky. We get a name. Charlie Lasher. We follow this up and we discover that this Charlie Lasher is supposed to sleep on a mattress in the same alley where Mary Sloan fucked up.

Eddie and I start a stake-out at the alleyway. Night after night, we wait in our unmarked car across from the alley. Nothing. In the car with me, I've got my sawed-off shotgun. I made it myself.

The seventh night, we're sitting in the dark, talking about a retirement party later for a second grade detective, Sammy Ryan, at Sally's Hi-Tide Restaurant. We wear out that subject, and I'm complaining again about Eddie smoking—I think he smokes rope—when we see somebody slip into the alley. It must be Lasher. We give him a few minutes, then we get out of the car.

I put two shells in the chambers of my shotgun. Number 4 Magnum, each holding twenty-eight ball bearings. They'll evaporate a person.

Moving real quiet, we go into the alley. In the glow of Eddie's flashlight, we can see this Lasher bedded down on an old mattress. He's not alone. All around him, stretched out, are about ten dogs.

This sonofabitch has been feeding these wild dogs, making buddies of them so they'll attack anybody he tells them to. He's got a pack of guard dogs, real vicious. We can also see all the garbage, the beer cans and the kitchen refuse and paper bags strewn along the alley and we can smell it, too.

I call out, "Charlie Lasher! We're the cops. Come on forward!" That does it.

Lasher jumps up from the mattress and he shouts at his pack of dogs, "Go get 'em! Get 'em!"

The dogs, all snarling and barking, turn on us, showing their teeth. Lasher runs for the wall at the end of the alley and begins to climb it. We can't get to him because the dogs are almost on us and they're mean enough to scare a lion tamer.

I like dogs . . . I've got one of my own . . . a German shepherd, Venus is her name . . . but this bastard is going to get away if we don't do something fast. I lower the muzzle of my shotgun at the dogs and I pull the trigger. Baroomph!

3

The explosion . . . Jesus! In the little alley, it sounds like a cannon.

The ball bearings rip into the dogs. Half a dozen of them collapse on the ground. There's a whole pile of dead and wounded dogs there. The others run off whimpering. Through the smoke from the barrel, I see Lasher. He's got a grip on the top of the wall.

We run forward past the bleeding, yelping dogs and I shout, "Go ahead, Charlie! Put your leg over that wall and I'll burn you. I've got another shot waiting for you. I'll kill you!" I'm ready to blow him apart, the bastard.

Lasher freezes. He drops back to the ground. "You've got me, man," he says. "Don't do it. Please don't do it." We put the cuffs on him.

When we leave the alley, we have to step over the corpses of Lasher's guard dogs. Blood all over the place, like a slaughterhouse.

"Man," Lasher says, "why did you have to kill my pets?" I don't say anything. I'm thinking this scene wasn't in the books or in the lectures when they trained me at the Police Academy.

We take him back to the 41st Precinct and we lock him up. By the time we've completed all the paperwork, we're very tired. We've been on duty all of one day and now it's 7 A.M. of the second day. Eddie and me, we look as if we've been to an all-night party.

Before we can take Lasher to court, we have to get this undercover dame around to the stationhouse to identify him. I call her and tell her we've got one of the guys who took her off.

I don't expect her to blow me kisses over the telephone, but neither do I expect her to blow her top, which is what she does. "That's my case," she screams. "What right have you got to arrest him? You shouldn't have picked him up. My team and me, we're working on that. We're taking care of it all."

I give her the most gentlemanly reply I can think of. "Bullshit," I say. "We've got him and you've gotta come down and identify him."

I know what it is. She wants to pick up the suspects herself, she and her team. They've already grabbed one guy and they want to get the other two. They don't want a couple of robbery detectives doing their job for them.

What she doesn't realize is, I've been assigned to the case. It's a robbery and that's my department. There's a lot more shouting and arguing, but finally she agrees to come to my office. She says she'll be down at 9 A.M. so we can go to pre-arraignment.

At 10 A.M. she still hasn't shown. Instead, we get a telephone call from the Narcotics Bureau. It's a captain and he says, "What the hell is going on? Mary Sloan says you're screwing up her case."

I tell him what happened and then he tells me what this crazy policewoman has done. After putting down the phone on me, she decides to complain to her boss, the commander of Narcotics. The thing is, he's not in New York. He's at a conference in Washington, D.C.

This doesn't stop her. She makes a long-distance call to him and puts in this big complaint that Detective Anthony Schiano is interfering with her case. The commander calls the Narcotics Bureau and tells this captain to sort it out.

When I tell this captain that I'm the investigating officer, that my boss has ordered me to take the case, he says, "Okay, stay there. We'll be over."

5

Again we wait and now it's noon and we've been on duty more than 24 hours straight. This captain, accompanied by a lieutenant and a couple of sergeants, comes in. They take me off to a room and start questioning me. I tell them the whole bit, all over again. As far as I'm concerned, this policewoman has got to be a psycho.

When I've done, they look at each other. They know as well as I do that it's my job to work this case, that if I hadn't pursued it, I'd have had some explaining to do to my boss. They shrug, and they decide to wait until Mary Sloan decides to make an appearance.

Finally, she comes waltzing in. I'm furious and so are the supervisors from the Narcotics Bureau. They don't like hanging around any more than I do. But she couldn't care less.

We put Lasher in a line-up and, through a one-way glass, Mary Sloan identifies him. While she's looking at him, I'm looking at her and I'm thinking. I'm thinking that dealing with a nutty policewoman wasn't in the training at the Police Academy, either.

There are a lot of things they don't teach at the Academy. How to give a summons, how to testify, unarmed combat, the law . . . they gave us all that. But they couldn't teach you to control your bowels when you're going up a dark staircase with a gun in your hand, how to deal with a bar fight, how to fight a pack of wild dogs or how to react to a woman cop who's jealous because another cop caught the guy who mugged her.

Of course, none of those problems were in my mind when I first got the idea of becoming a cop. It was in the winter months of 1953. I'm riding the subway when I see a guy across the aisle reading a newspaper. I happen to see a headline. It says that 13,000 applicants are going to take a police examination. I start to daydream. I see myself in the uniform, with a gun at my hip. I see myself arresting murderers and crooks. I see myself getting medals.

But then I tell myself I could never make it. Not with my background of East Harlem and gang fights and petty crime. Besides, I think, I'm not big enough. To me, a cop has to be big and tough and intelligent. I'm just a skinny, 21-year-old kid from a broken home, earning $40 a week in the latest of a succession of dead-end jobs.

I talk to my cousin Gene Spago, who works for the fire department. He tells me I should take the examination. Where I come from, it's a big deal getting a job with the city.

To prepare myself for the examination, I do a lot of studying. Then the day comes. I go to a high school on Fordham Road in the Bronx. There's hundreds of guys there, waiting to take the written test, drinking coffee and bullshitting.

I go to a fourth-floor classroom and when I sit down at a desk, I see a pamphlet with maybe a hundred pages in it and a pencil. The man in charge says we're not to open the pamphlets until the bell goes. Each of us has to have his thumbprint taken. This is to stop any phonies taking the test for somebody else.

When the bell sounds, the man says, "Okay, open the pamphlet. You have four hours to complete the questions."

I'm very nervous as I look at the questions. They're not easy. But I do my best.

A month later I get a letter from the city. I know this is it, one way or another. I make the sign of the cross and open it. I've passed—just. I get 78 points. The passing mark is 75.

Now I've got to go to Van Cortlandt Park to take the physical test, bringing with me a pair of sneakers, shorts and sweat shirt.

We're tested on running, climbing, jumping and lifting

7

weights. I notice I'm the smallest of the guys trying out—5 feet, 9½ inches, and 134 pounds. But where some of them can only lift a 25-pound weight over their heads, I lift an 80-pound weight, which is 100 per cent. For the whole test, I get over 95 points.

Sometime later, I get another letter from the city saying I've been accepted in the New York Police Department, pending an investigation of my background. The investigation, I think, could be the toughest of all the tests.

I have to report to a Sergeant Ableman at the 23rd Precinct. Ableman is a semi-bald fellow in his early forties. He seems like a nice guy. He's sitting in a dark little office with my portfolio on his desk. He gives me a list of all the records he wants from me—my school records, the address of any house I ever lived in, my army records, a description of any car I ever owned, details of any job I ever had and an explanation of what I was doing if I didn't have a job.

"Have you ever been in trouble with the police?" Ableman asks.

I'm thinking of the times in East Harlem when the cops have grabbed me on minor things and taken my name. I can see the whole thing going out the window.

"No," I reply.

He knows, of course. Later, he tells me the police records show me as a juvenile delinquent for opening fire hydrants in the summer and driving cars without a license. But apparently it's not bad enough to kill my chances with the police department.

I think this Ableman understands how important it is to me to become a cop. I think he likes my eagerness, the way I keep asking when I can start training. He tells me that some of the applicants, guys who did better in the examinations, aren't as enthusiastic as me.

Finally, the letter comes. I've been accepted as a member of the police department. Wow! My dad kisses me, and Gene Spago, my cousin, he's as pleased as if I've won on the numbers. The letter tells me to report to the chief clerk's office at police headquarters on Center Street to pick up my badge.

There's a bunch of us there to be sworn in. We raise our right hands and promise to uphold law and order. We form a line and as we walk out, we pass a man with a large box.

He gives each of us a yellow envelope. Inside is a silver badge. I look at it and at the number on it—9947. I smile. Patrolman Anthony Schiano, shield number 9947. It sounds pretty neat.

That night, when I go to bed, I pin the badge on my pajamas. I march into the room where my dad's sitting reading the paper and I say, "Mr. Schiano, you're under arrest!" He looks up at me and he grins. He gets up and he embraces the arresting officer because he knows how proud I feel and I guess he's pretty proud of me. The badge is still on my pajamas when I get up in the morning.

Next, I have to go down to the Equipment Bureau on Broome Street, across from police headquarters. There's a couple of hundred of us. We file in and are given a hat with the police insignia, a gun belt and holster, and handcuffs.

We get a leather memo-pad holder and the gray uniform of a probationary patrolman.

We're given a choice of a Colt, or Smith and Wesson revolver. I choose the .38 Colt. A patrolman stamps my shield number onto the butt of the gun. At the end of the line, we come to a cashier's window. We don't have to pay anything now, but we're told we'll have to pay the $385 we owe for our equipment from later pay checks.

When I get home, I put on my grays and adjust my hat

to the best John Wayne angle. I try it forward, well over the eyes. I try it back, sort of relaxed. I try it at an angle, dashing and suave. I strap on my gun and confront myself in the mirror. "Okay, mister," I say, drawing my gun, "you're under arrest. Don't try anything on me." I have to admit I'm not exactly John Wayne, but it'll have to do.

Next day, I'm ordered to go to the Inter-City Blood Bank on 152nd Street. They take a pint of blood from me. I'm still a bit irritated about that. I didn't volunteer to give blood. They just told me to go there and they took the blood.

January 10, 1955, I start at the Police Academy. In those days, it was a grimy, fly-blown old building that used to be an elementary school. It was on Hubert Street in Lower Manhattan. At 8:30 in the morning, it didn't look good. For that matter, at any time it wouldn't look good.

We're split up into classes. Because of my height, they put me in Class 21 with all the shorter guys. We're all looking at each other and wondering how we're going to make out together.

Right off, I can tell that some of them are street guys like me. One of them, Frankie Vine, comes from my neighborhood, East 108th Street. He's tough and street-smart, an ex-pug older than most of us. I think to myself, ah, a wise guy. Another one, Larry Transito, lives with his mother who keeps a candy store on Second Avenue, around 122nd Street. He's another tough one, an abrupt, boisterous guy who also comes across as a wise guy.

Like me, they talk rough because that's the language of East Harlem. Like me, they've played stickball off the stoops of the tenements and stolen hub caps and grabbed candy from the corner store when nobody's looking.

As kids, we'd never rat on anybody to the police. The cops were our enemies. A gambler, a racketeer, even a dope pusher . . . they got more respect than the cops and you'd never tell the cops anything about them. Right or wrong, that's the way it was.

The three of us, we become good friends. We stand in line for the roll call and I can hear Frankie Vine giving the bosses a razz. From the ranks comes his growl, "Bullshit . . ." This upsets the instructors.

"Listen to me, you men," one of them says. "You're not out on the street now. You're police officers of the city of New York. If you don't have respect for the instructors and what they're teaching you, you might as well leave now.

"You can either work and pass through the Academy or you can refuse discipline and get flopped."

Another of the probationary patrolmen I make friends with is a big black guy called Johnny Manson.

He's one of the last of the group to join the Academy. He should have gone to one of the classes with the tall fellows, but they're all filled up so he ends up in our class of shorties. They call us the pygmy class.

After roll call, we march off to our classes. Everything has to be done by the numbers, like West Point, although there's nothing else similar between West Point and Hubert Street. Our instructor is a Sergeant Smee, with glasses, reddish hair and a squeaky voice like Wally Cox.

"All right, fellows," he squeaks, "you are policemen. You will follow orders. If you cross me, if I catch you cheating, if I catch you disobeying the rules, you will be dismissed.

"If you get a certain amount of demerits, you'll have to do the whole Academy training all over again."

The squeaky voice is too much for Frankie Vine. From his desk comes, "Ho, ho, ho!" That starts off a whole lot of snickering.

"All right, wise guys," the sergeant squeaks, "for my first

punishment, you step up." He points to Frankie, who shambles forward moving his shoulders just like a boxer walking into the ring. I grin, thinking about my old bopping gang, the Italian Dukes. They'd have accepted Frankie immediately.

"What you're gonna do," Smee squeaks, "is you're gonna go outside and mop the hallways. If you don't want to do that, you'll be tossed out of the Academy."

Frankie turns around, smirks at the class and walks out to find a mop.

Sergeant Smee tells us to take out the books which we picked up with our equipment. These are books on first aid, the penal law, the criminal code, vehicle traffic law, and so on. But first he gives us a lecture on the psychology of the cop on the street.

He tells us why we're on the street, how people are going to regard us, how we're different now from ordinary people, how our only real friends from now on will be other policemen.

"A policeman is like a doctor or a priest," he says. "It's almost like being a member of a religious order. People are going to look at you differently from now on. And you've got to be worthy of their respect."

He tells us about our memo books, that we must write down anything of significance. He warns us not to take any action on the street as probationary patrolmen unless absolutely necessary. He tells us that we must be home by midnight, what he calls "the bewitching hour."

One of the wise guys chirps up, "Why, sergeant? Do we turn into pumpkins otherwise?"

Sergeant Smee is feeling good, I guess, because now it's lunchtime so he just calls us a bunch of wise guys and squeaks out that we're dismissed to get lunch.

After lunch, we have to report to the armory at 34th Street and Park Avenue for a class in physical combat and gun practice. Johnny Manson, Frankie Vine and me, we decide to catch a bus. It's occurred to the three of us that this will be the first time we can ride a bus without paying because now we're patrolmen under training.

We let other people waiting at the bus stop climb on board first. Then we grin at each other and walk past the driver without paying. It's great. We see there are half a dozen other guys from the Academy already on board. We sit down and start talking about our first day at the Academy. The bus stops again and more people come on board. There aren't enough seats and two of them have to stand.

Holy mackerel, I think. They're paying passengers having to stand and here we all are sitting down without paying. Johnny Manson and me, we stand up to give them our seats.

Immediately, all the other probationary patrolmen stand up, so now there are half a dozen empty seats. Johnny and I slip into a couple of the seats the other guys have left empty. Then they all rush to sit down as well but of course a couple are left standing.

At the next stop, more people come on board and again all of us guys in gray get to our feet. And so it goes until we reach the armory. We're all grinning at it all and so are the passengers.

We go to the firing range which consists of about fifteen booths, with targets set up at a range of twenty-five yards. An instructor gives us a lecture. He warns us how dangerous a gun can be and emphasizes that we must never draw ours unless there's no other way out.

Because they go in alphabetical order and my name begins with an S, I'm one of the last to fire. By the time I take my place in one of the booths, my ears are ringing from the explosions that have been roaring from the guns of my class-mates.

The instructor says, "Okay, Schiano, load five in your chambers." I slip five .38 bullets into my brand-new service revolver.

I point the gun at the target and take careful aim. I'm just squeezing the trigger, nice and steady, when the guy next to me fires. "Baroomph!" it goes, right in my ear. It upsets me so much that I give a little jump as I'm firing my shot. I peer after it and see that my target has disappeared. It's disap-peared because I hit the metal stand holding the target and knocked the whole thing over.

The instructor has to stop all the shooting so I can walk forward and put my target back in place. Again I aim, but now I'm real nervous and I don't do well. Later, I become a sharpshooter, then a marksman, then finally an expert.

As the days go by at the Academy, we discover just how dry and boring the law can be. We have to learn the administrative code, the code of criminal procedures, the penal law. We have to understand the difference between robbery first degree, robbery second degree, robbery third degree. The various degrees of burglary and every other crime. The difference between sexual assault and rape. Loitering for various reasons. Narcotics. We're told that when we go out on the street, we must be able to determine which category every crime falls into.

We're told that the job of a police officer is to protect the life and property of the people. That's the basic task of the cop. Everything we do comes from that. And we begin to realize how much paperwork, filling in forms, is involved in protecting the life and property of the people.

A couple of weeks after joining the Academy, I get my first outside assignment. I'm told to report to the commanding officer of the 22nd Precinct at Central Park for a 4 P.M. to 10 P.M. tour. I arrive at the stationhouse, march over to the desk officer and stand at attention in front of him. He's busy and he doesn't see me. Patrolmen are coming in and out. They see me standing stiffly at attention in front of the desk, and they grin at each other.

At last the desk officer looks up from his papers and says, "What d'you want?" I give him a snappy salute which he doesn't bother to return. "Lieutenant," I say, "I'm probationary patrolman Anthony Schiano from the Police Academy, reporting to duty as ordered."

"Oh, yeah, yeah, I know," he says. "I'll get around to you in a minute. Stand over there."

When he gets around to me, he says, "Okay, kid, d'you know how to handle the telephone switchboard?"

"Yes, sir," I say, although I'm not too sure. They taught us a bit about a switchboard at the Academy, but not much.

"You go and relieve the patrolman over there," he says.

I take over the switchboard and start handling calls. "Probationary patrolman Schiano, 22nd Precinct," I say to callers. "Can I help you?"

At first, it goes well and I'm pretty pleased with myself, plugging in calls and connecting people. But then it gets busy. The board starts to light up and I find I'm crossing wires. Everything gets fouled up.

A detective comes down from the squad room and yells, "Who the hell is handling that switchboard? First I'm talking to a complainant and then suddenly I'm talking to a crazy Chinaman." Other cops come charging down, complaining about the switchboard. I'm in a panic.

The lieutenant looks at me, sighs, and says, "Okay, get out of there. Go wait in the back." Eventually, they decide to try me on clerical work. They tell me to sit at a desk and put carbon between two sheets of paper. My first time out of the Academy, me with a badge on my chest that says I'm a member of the New York Police Department, and I'm sitting putting carbons between papers. I'm glad when the tour ends.

The next outside assignment is to Traffic B at the 18th Precinct. I'm going to direct traffic. That's better than fiddling with carbon paper in a back room.

They team me up with a seasoned patrolman called Greenthal, whose post is the intersection of 45th Street and Broadway.

While I'm waiting for the roll call, I hang around with the patrolmen in the muster room and listen to their conversations. They're talking about the arrests they've made and which are the bad bosses. I hear one patrolman talking about a restaurant he's been to where he tips the waitress twenty-five cents and that's all he pays for a three-dollar meal.

Greenthal and me, we take a bus to 45th and Broadway. He asks which neighborhood I come from and if I've done traffic duty before. He's about 6 feet tall, 180 pounds, and he's been on the job about fifteen years. He says he likes a quiet life. He doesn't want to be anything but a patrolman and he doesn't mind doing traffic duty because then he doesn't have to work late at night.

"I wouldn't mind being a detective," I venture. "That must be fun. Or, better still, if I could get into the aviation section because I did some flying in Korea in the army."

"Forget it, kid," he says. "You'll never make the aviation bureau or the detective bureau. You gotta have a hook. You gotta know the mayor or some senior officer to get in something like that.

"If you become a detective, you'll wind up in the gutter with a bullet in your back."

I tell him, "Listen, Greenthal, if I want something, I go for it." I guess I'm a bit excited.

"Relax, kid," he says, "take it easy. Don't make waves."

"Okay, okay," I say. "I'm just excited at the thought of being at the intersection directing traffic."

"Excited at traffic duty?" he says, and he raises his eyes to heaven. "Listen, all we do is stand in the middle of the intersection and let people see us. We don't do anything. We let the traffic lights do it all."

When we reach our post, the traffic is building up. It's early Sunday evening and all the moviegoers and tourists are filling Broadway. We go and stand in the middle of the intersection and I look around at the flashing, bright lights and all the people and the traffic and I feel pretty good.

Everything is going smoothly and after about an hour, Greenthal, looking at his watch, says, "I'm going to have my meal now. I'll be in that restaurant over there. You get over there to the corner of the intersection and stand there so people can see you. Don't move from the corner. Don't do anything."

I stand on the corner for a while and then I think, what the hell, I'm supposed to be on traffic duty, so that's what I'll do. I move back out to the middle of the intersection and now I feel I'm in control of the whole situation. I like it when people walking across the street with the lights say, "Hello, officer." I like people looking at me in my gray uniform.

I see a couple of kids, unruly-looking suspicious-seeming characters and I think back to when I was like them, out for

17

trouble in the Times Square area. I look like a kid myself, in spite of the uniform, but they see me watching them and they turn down a side street. My chest swells up. They know who's boss.

I take out my whistle. I've had it a while now but I've never blown it, not officially. When the lights change, I give a blast on it. It's terrific. The traffic does just what my whistle tells it to.

But then along comes this old guy in a beat-up jalopy, trying to make a turn. Right in the middle of the intersection, he stalls.

I go over, the cop in charge. I tell him, "Mister, you gotta move that car."

"I can't," he says. "The battery's dead."

The traffic is starting to pile up. Stupid drivers are blowing their horns.

"Turn off your lights," I say. "Don't kill the battery."

Pedestrians are gathering. One wise guy's roaring with laughter. "Hey, officer," he says, "d'you want me to call a cop?"

I'm scurrying around, trying to get traffic to back away from the stalled car, but it's hopeless. As far as I can see, there's buses and cars and trucks jammed together bumper to bumper. The stinking old car won't start. I blow my whistle but that just adds to the noise.

In the restaurant, Greenthal is digging into his big meal when the noise from outside begins to percolate. He hears horns and he sees people pointing through the windows of the café. He looks out and he sees me almost lost in a sea of jammed vehicles, frantically trying to sort it out.

He has to abandon his meal, pull his overcoat on and come charging out. The only trouble is he can't reach me. He has

18

to climb over the hoods of cars and, in one case, open the back door of a taxi and come out the other. I see him coming and I don't feel good. His coat is open because he had no time to button it up and he's fuming.

"What the fuck is going on?" he says. "I leave you for a couple of minutes and you bring the city to a halt!" Even with the noise of the horns and people shouting, I can still hear every syllable. He's talking quite loud. "Didn't I tell you to stand on that corner and do nothing? Didn't I?" Actually, he's shouting.

I tell him, "I felt foolish just standing on the corner. I thought I should direct the traffic. And then this guy stalled in the middle of the intersection. I had to do something. Besides, I wanted to blow my whistle."

"You wanted to blow your whistle!"

"Yeah. I never blew my whistle before."

He slaps his thigh, he's so mad. "I give up," he says. "Come on, let's push this guy out of the way." We start trying to get the broken-down car out of the traffic. Eventually, we get it over to a bus stop and he starts to tackle the traffic jam. It takes him nearly an hour and a half.

"Listen," he says. "Go and eat. But while you're going to eat, don't do nothing. Don't lift a finger. Just walk quietly over to that restaurant and eat. Don't take no action. Don't make any arrests. Don't spit. Don't look at anybody. Don't give anybody any directions. Don't do nothing. Got it?"

The next day at the Academy, all the guys are talking about their assignments the day before. One guy says he worked a switchboard at a stationhouse. Another says he actually walked a post in Harlem. Other fellows say they rode in radio cars.

I tell them I directed traffic on Broadway at 45th. I don't

tell them all about it. In fact, I say I did a very good job. They're quite impressed.

At the Academy, one of my favorite classes is a sort of play entitled, "Patrolman Right and Patrolman Wrong." It's to teach us how to give a summons to a motorist the right way and the wrong way. It's also supposed to teach us to be honest.

On the stage, you have a couple of ordinary seasoned patrolmen, one of them playing the part of a motorist. The other patrolman stops him for a traffic offense and says, for instance, "Sir, you have just passed a red light. May I have your license and registration?"

The driver says, "Sorry, officer, I was in a hurry." Then he winks as he hands over his wallet. If it's Patrolman Wrong, he winks back and leans on the car window while he goes through the wallet. Between the license and the registration, he finds a five dollar bill.

Patrolman Wrong surreptitiously palms the money and returns the wallet. "Sir, he says. "You can go this time. Be more careful in the future."

If it's Patrolman Right, he refuses to take the wallet. He says, "Please, no, sir. Take your license and registration from the wallet and hand them to me."

When Patrolman Right finds the five dollar bill, he says, "Sir, I'm now placing you under arrest for attempted bribery. Please come with me to the stationhouse." We all would give Patrolman Right a big round of applause.

After classes one day, I go to the 86th Street Orpheum to see Edward G. Robinson in "I Am the Law." The title appeals to me. I'm sitting there in my gray uniform, engrossed in the movie, when I feel a draft around my groin.

I look down and I see my fly is open. Next to me is a guy with a big shit-eating grin on his mug. He's giving me the eye.

I grab him by the throat, pick him up and drag him outside to the manager's office. There's a woman there and she sees me in my uniform and she gets the picture because my zipper is still open.

She calls the police but she doesn't say it right. She says, "Please send over some help—there's a patrolman in trouble." It goes out over the air as "Assist patrolman—10–13."

Now, if a message like that goes over the air in New York City, get out of the way of a cop. That's the priority message for all officers. I hear the radio cars coming, so I take my prisoner out to the street. The woman goes to collect my schoolbag.

While I'm waiting under the marquee, the patrol cars race up. One comes right up onto the sidewalk and halfway into the movie house entrance, all the way to the door. In a couple of minutes, ten other radio cars are there, half of them mounted on the sidewalk.

Boy, am I embarrassed. The cavalry to the rescue—and all for a little fag. But that's not the end of it.

Periodically, at the Academy, our commander gave a speech in the auditorium on the procedures of police work, our duties and responsibilities. Always he told us not to take any action in the street unless it was absolutely necessary. We were still not full-fledged patrolmen. Sometimes, however, he introduced probationary patrolmen who had done something worthy.

The commander says, "This probationary patrolman made an arrest for robbery." Or he says, "This officer arrested a suspect in a burglary case." All of us give out with a big round of applause. One guy has saved a kid from drowning in a pool in Central Park and he gets a thunderous ovation.

I'm called onto the stage. The commander tells all my

brothers officers that I've made an arrest—of a fag in a movie house. The guys in the auditorium, they give me the razz, whistling and laughing and giving me mock cheers. I'm glad to get off that stage. But they're just having fun. I get on with them pretty well.

Towards the end of my time at the Academy, my marks get bad, very bad. Book learning is not my thing and I'm spending too much time with my girl Helen. Sergeant Smee begins to keep me after class. "Probationary Schiano," he says, "you know your marks have been terrible and they're getting steadily worse.

"You know what it proves, Schiano? It proves you'll never amount to anything. I understand you come from East Harlem, around 116th Street?"

"Yes, sir, I do."

"Yeah, well, I think you'll probably be dropped from the department within the first nine months' probation period. Even if you stay on the job, you'll just wind up as a sweeper in a stationhouse. You'd better get on the ball. Dismissed."

I leave the room, swearing to myself that one day I'll make him eat his words—which is probably what he wants me to do. I pull myself together and I start to get better marks.

The week before graduation, we get circulars asking us which precincts we'd like to be assigned to. We'd discussed this among ourselves, and I decide I want the 18th Precinct, Midtown Manhattan, because I think this will be very exciting, the Times Square area, the theater district and movie houses. To me, this is glamorous. Also, a policeman gets into a movie on the arm. This isn't a case of the movie owner losing the price of a ticket. He wants the cop in his movie house.

When the cop walks into the movie, the manager asks him

where he's going to sit, because if there's any trouble he knows he can call on that cop for help. But the main thing for me is the idea of bright lights and action in the heart of the city.

My second and third choices are the 45th and 50th Precincts in the Bronx, mainly because they're close to the home of my girl Helen. Talking to the other guys, I learn that most of them have asked for the midtown Manhattan precinct. My black partner, Johnny Manson, he wants midtown, too.

The night before graduation I can't sleep. I clean my uniform and equipment and go to bed. I get up and clean it again. I've even got blue jockey shorts and a blue T-shirt to wear under the uniform, and they're as well-pressed as everything else. I've had a real close haircut, which is a mistake because I find my cap slips down until it rests on my ears.

April 6, 1955—the big day.

I get up and put on my blue uniform, my gun, my hat and I look into the mirror. Ech! I want to look like a seasoned cop, but I don't. I've got no behind and the pants look baggy, like a clown's. The choker jacket is cutting into my neck. The hat is slipping down over my eyes. I look like a skinny kid who's dressed up for a costume party.

If I don't impress myself, how am I going to impress people when I walk my post?

I give myself a final disgusted look and go down to join my parents. They're separated, but they get together for my graduation. Off we go in a cab to City College, where the ceremony is to be held.

The classes are forming up on the ball field. We all shake hands, Johnny Manson and Frankie Vine and Larry Transito and a fellow named Bill Poster who later becomes my commanding officer when I'm a detective. There's a smell of fresh-cut grass. All our relatives are in the stands, looking down at us as we fall in under the bright spring sunshine. I see that the other fellows, at least, look smart in their pressed blues and white gloves.

After some speeches, we line up and march onto the platform, salute and are handed envelopes containing our first assignments. When we form up again on the ball field, we are real, live, honest-to-God, full-fledged policemen. We can't wait to open our envelopes.

I look at the piece of paper in mine. It says I'm to be assigned as a patrolman to the 32nd Precinct. Where the hell is the 32nd Precinct? It sure as hell isn't midtown.

The other guys tell me. It's Harlem. Not my East Harlem, but black Harlem on the West Side. Frankie Vine and Larry Transito, they get the same precinct. Here is one of the toughest areas in New York City and they're sending guys from the pygmy class there. Some of the fellows say, "Wow, that's a big money precinct. There's a lot of gambling and policy operations up there."

During my days at the Academy some of the cadets, particularly those with relatives on the job, had talked of bribery and gratuities for ignoring gambling. As I look around the ball field, I can see some guys who've talked about making money as a policeman, taking advantage of their badge. Me and my buddies, we'd hear this kind of talk and we'd look at each other and shake our heads. That wasn't what we'd become cops for. Later on, I find that these are the guys who get arrested for taking bribes, the guys who make the whole department look bad.

A bunch of us decide to go and celebrate at a restaurant downtown. I have the same feeling about these guys that I had when I was with my buddies in the army. I know I'd do anything for them and I know they'd do the same for me.

That night, my father is waiting for me. He wants to talk.

He tells me about how he comes to this country to make a new life. He tells me that always he's known racketeers. Guys like Joe Valachi, who used to hang around 116th Street and Pleasant Avenue. My dad, as a house painter in the area, had to live with these hoods in order to survive.

He talks about the cops in the neighborhood, some of them on the take from the mobsters. I nod because I've seen these cops, shaking hands with hoods and taking money from them on street corners.

My dad is very serious. He points a finger at me and he says, "Remember, my son, when you go on the street, nobody buys you off. It's not because you might get caught and go to jail. You must never take, because if you do you're selling your integrity, you're selling yourself. You've got to be a man, and nobody buys off a man. Nobody buys off Patrolman Anthony Schiano."

That's what I'm thinking as I go to bed.

2

THE 32nd Precinct is on West 135th Street, in the heart of Harlem. I get off the subway at St. Nicholas Avenue and walk east. Nearly every face on the street is black. I've never been in any all-black neighborhood like this without my gang. Although I was at this stationhouse once—in handcuffs. But things are changing for me now.

On every corner, it seems, there's a bar or a liquor store. This alone tells me I've arrived in a precinct where there's plenty of action.

I'm wearing civilian clothes, carrying my uniform on a hanger covered with cellophane. The big gray stationhouse is easily spotted. It's not impressive but it looks official. There's a flag hanging outside and two green lights at the entrance saying "32nd Precinct." Other guys carrying uniforms on hangers are walking in.

Feeling like a new boy at school, I climb the steps and enter. There's a big room, with bright lights burning even though it's daytime. Ahead of me is a large blackboard showing chalked messages telling some patrolmen to report to a certain sergeant and telling others to turn in summonses. It means nothing to me.

To the left are three doors, one with the words "Com-

26

manding officer, 32nd Precinct." Also on the left is a big showcase holding trophies won by the Precinct for baseball, softball, basketball and bowling.

To the right is an enormous wooden desk which faces a wrought-iron railing. Behind the desk, there's a lot of activity because the tour is changing. The desk officer is talking to another lieutenant who's about to relieve him.

The smell of the place . . . well, anybody who's been in a public school, a football changing room, or an army barracks would recognize it. It's mostly an absence of anything feminine, like decoration or scent or luxury. It's an institution, a place for rough men to do rough work.

The desk officer looks up at me standing there and he says, "Yes? Can I help you?"

"Patrolman Anthony Schiano," I say, "reporting for my first tour of duty."

"Fine," he says. "Hey, Johnson, show this guy where the locker room is."

Patrolman Johnson is a sweeper at the precinct. A sweeper cleans up and looks after the cells. Later, he becomes a good friend of mine, telling me all about the job. He's an immaculate black guy. He's got a real sharp haircut. His shoes glitter. He's wearing well-pressed dark gray slacks and a dark blue police shirt, with his badge pinned to it. His nails are manicured. He's so clean, he looks as though he'd scrubbed himself with Brillo.

"This guy's a sweeper?" I think. "He looks and smells more like a movie star."

He tells me that at one time he worked on gambling in the chief inspector's office. The scuttlebutt was that you made something like $2,500 a month in that job. This guy, according to rumor, is a millionaire. They say he got out of the chief inspector's office just before a big scandal broke and that he lost himself in the 32nd Precinct. All he wants is to be forgotten until he can retire.

I don't know about that. I do know that he acts like a father towards me. Over and over again, he warns me to stay away from graft. "It's no good," he says. "Be honest and do your best and then you'll have no worries. Take bribes and you spend all your life worrying you'll be caught. It's no way to live."

This first day, in the locker room while I'm putting on my uniform, he tells me which of the guys in the street are taking horse bets and policy bets. "Stay away from them," he says. "They're trouble. Another thing, motorists around here, they'll try and give you money to forget traffic offenses. Don't buy it. You'll only get into trouble." The guy sounds just like the instructors at the Police Academy.

I go down to the patrolmen's sitting room and look in the alarm book, which consists of teletype messages reporting the current crimes throughout the five boroughs . . . stolen vehicles, missing persons, robberies, killings, and so on. I write down in the back of my memo book all the numbers of stolen cars.

The other patrolmen know I'm new on the job. They're friendly. They show me the roll call which lists the post I'm to walk. I see I have a school crossing. My mealtime is there. So is the time I have to call in to the stationhouse, one minute after the hour, every hour.

A sergeant calls us to attention and we fall in, forty or fifty men, in lines of three, to answer to our names. I notice that most of the patrolmen are white. While the sergeant is giving instructions, I look up and see framed photographs of cops who were killed in the line of duty in the 32nd Precinct.

We're marched out to line up in front of the desk officer, and the commanding officer walks around to face us. He's a slim, dark-haired guy with a cool smile on his face. This is Captain Sampson, and I soon learn about him.

While he was a patrolman, he was assigned to a precinct in Queens as a clerical man. One night, a drunken policeman in full uniform came staggering into the stationhouse. He'd walked off his post.

The drunk started shouting for the commanding officer of this Queens precinct. The commander heard the commotion and came out of his office. The drunken cop drew his revolver and shot the commanding officer. Dead.

Sampson drew his gun and he shot the drunken patrolman, killing him just as he was about to get off another shot at other officers.

Now, years later, this Sampson is my commanding officer. He talks to us about the various infractions we must watch out for and then he steps back and the sergeant says, "Take your posts."

With two other patrolmen, I set off for my post, West 138th Street, between Fifth Avenue, Lenox Avenue and Seventh Avenue. It's a pretty day, cool with a nice clear sky, and I realize I've got a silly smile on my face. I feel good. By the time I reach my post, my buddies have peeled off to their own areas.

The patrolman I'm relieving can't wait to get back to the stationhouse, and home. That's okay by me. With him gone, I'm at long last a patrolman on post, ready to catch criminals, help citizens in distress, see that the law is obeyed. A guardian of justice.

I stand on the corner of Seventh Avenue and 138th Street and look about, feeling benevolent about the street and the people . . . my street, my people. Of course, that doesn't mean I'm going to be benevolent towards any crooks or lawbreakers. At the thought of them, I try to look tough, but the trouble is I know I still look like a skinny kid dressed up as a cop.

I feel better when a woman comes up and asks for directions. At least she can tell I'm a cop. Even so, I get the idea she knows I'm a rookie because she gives me this motherly smile. I wonder if she can smell the mothballs on my uniform.

Walking east towards Lenox Avenue, I try swinging my nightstick like the seasoned cops do, with that casual touch, nice and easy. It doesn't do what it's supposed to. I've tried it before and I just can't get the hang of it. I give up.

It's not a bad street, relatively clean and respectable. As I stroll along, I see a guy standing outside a five-story tenement building. He's in his late fifties and he's wearing a brown fedora.

People approach him, talk to him, pass by him into the hallway and then leave. He seems a very happy guy, smiling and nodding at all the people going in and out. I wonder what's going on, but when I get to him, he just nods and smiles, so I nod and smile at him and on I go. At this time, I don't know much about betting on the numbers. It's one of Harlem's main sports.

It's fairly early in the morning, so although this is supposed to be a tough neighborhood, there's plenty of traffic and pedestrians bustling about. Women are setting off for the shops and men are heading for work. Kids, running off to school, shout, "Hi, cop! Hi, cop!"

On the south side of the street, there's no parking at this hour. But I spot one lone car standing outside a church, a big gray building called the Abyssinian Baptist Church. It's an expensive-looking English sports car, a Jaguar. I remember one of the veteran patrolmen told me, "Before you give out a summons for parking, walk around the auto a bit to give the owner a chance to move it. If he shows up real quick, let him drive it off and don't give him a ticket."

I walk around the car, giving the owner a break. After all, it's my first day on the job. After a couple of minutes of me staring at the car and walking around it and staring at it again, a guy comes out from the church.

"Officer," he says, "you know whose car that is, don't you?"

"No, sir," I say, "I don't."

"That's the car of the Reverend Adam Clayton Powell."

"Oh,"

"You know him?" he asks.

"So?"

"Well, not only is he a reverend, but he is the congressman for this district."

"That's fine. Now, would you just ask the congressman to move his car so that the Sanitation Department can clean the street? Otherwise, I'll have to give him a ticket."

"I don't think he's gonna like that."

"Well, I'll tell you something, pal," I say. "If he's not out here in a couple of seconds, he's gonna get a summons. And if he's not out in the next ten minutes, I'm gonna make arrangements to have his auto towed away."

"You just hold your water, officer," he says, and he waltzes back into the church. Nothing happens. I stare at the church. I look at the car. I take another walk around the car. Nothing happens. I take out my memo book, which holds the blank summons, and I start to write out a ticket for the car.

Just as I complete the summons, the church door opens and out comes a very tall, smartly dressed guy. He's something. He's well over six foot and he has wavy black hair. He's got a handsome mug, light skin and blue or gray eyes. He's got a slim mustache. His clothes . . . forget it. He's wearing an English tweed coat with a black velvet collar. He smells of cologne and money.

He gets into the car. I go to him, tearing off the summons and handing it to him. "I'm sorry, sir," I say. "You know you were in violation." To tell the truth, I'm a bit awed by this swell with the expensive car and his important position. I'm betting this doesn't happen to him often.

"Officer," he says, "I know you're doing your job. Don't worry about it." And he takes the summons and drives off with a roar from the powerful engine.

I continue walking my post. A bit further on, I notice a "No Parking" sign has fallen off its pole.

I pick up the sign and place it against a wall on the ground. I make an entry in my memo book and then I call the stationhouse and report it. I'm taking it pretty seriously.

The patrolman on the switchboard at the 32nd Precinct seems to think I'm some kind of a nut. He says I'm the first officer who's ever reported that a "No Parking" sign is off its pole. Especially in the 32nd Precinct, which is a combat precinct. The guy on the switchboard leaves me with the impression that I should just be happy the sign isn't being used as a murder weapon.

Later, I call in again, this time to report I've found a parked car without license plates. I request a tow truck. But as I put the phone down, a fellow comes up and says it's his car and he's just about to have it towed away himself.

While I'm talking to him, a patrol car from the precinct

32

rolls up and an officer sticks his head out the window. "What you got, kid?" he demands. "A stolen car?" My face gets a bit red and I have to tell him the owner has shown up. He raises his eyebrows at me and drives off.

At midafternoon, my tour is over and I'm relieved from my post to return to the stationhouse and sign off. Before I go home, however, I decide to take a peek at the detective squad room.

In one corner is a cage containing some prisoners. They're making a lot of noise. A sharp-looking detective, well-dressed, with a cigar sticking out of his mouth, is questioning a man in handcuffs. I like the look of these detectives and I find myself daydreaming about the time when I'll be playing Sherlock Holmes.

One of the detectives turns to me and says, "Hello, kid. What can we do for you?"

"Just watching," I mutter.

"Oh," he says, "come by any time." I thank him, change into my civilian clothes and go home. As the days go by, I do different tours of duty. Either it's 8 A.M. to 4 P.M. or 4 P.M. to midnight, or midnight to 8 A.M. I learn about taking a piss on duty. You can go to any bathroom you fancy except a licensed premise. If you go to a bar to take a leak, you'd better make damn sure you enter it in your memo book, otherwise if you're spotted you can be in trouble.

Before every tour, there's a roll call. All the patrolmen gather in the sitting room. The sergeant comes in and bangs the table with his nightstick. We put on our coats and line up ready to march out in front of the desk where the commanding officer will look us over. The sergeant reads out our names to make sure we're all present.

He assigns us to our different posts or to radio cars. Then,

33

it's "Forward, march!" And we march into the muster room and form up in front of the desk at attention, our nightsticks in our right hands. Sometimes, the commanding officer reads off the roll call again. Sometimes, the sergeant just reports, "All present and accounted for except Roscoe, not present for duty," and that's that.

The commanding officer will brief us on conditions on our posts. He might say there's a traffic problem at a junction on one post. He might say there's gamblers in a certain hallway and we should put in a slip, noting that the address is "suspected premises." In such a case, we wouldn't try to do anything about it because our uniforms would warn the gamblers. That would be left to the plainclothes detail. The commanding officer might tell us to stay away from one area because plainclothes men or undercover agents are operating there and a uniformed man might screw up their operation.

On post, I look out for cars parked in violation. I look out for any hazards, such as glass on the street or, maybe, a trash can tipped over. I look up the superintendent of the building and tell him to get it cleaned up. Maybe there's an old refrigerator on the street that kids could climb into and become trapped in. I tell the building superintendent to remove the door from the refrigerator.

Protect life and property. That's what we're there for. It's not only crime. We're available if people are in trouble, whether it's sickness or family squabbles or accidents.

I discover my post can be scary. One tour, midnight to 8 A.M., I'm walking my post at about 4 A.M., trying doors, looking into hallways to make sure no mugger is lying up there, when I see a man trying to hide inside a doorway as I walk by. There's nobody else around. The streets are all wet with rain. I'm sweating a bit. This guy's shrinking back into the shadows. I wonder if he's packing a weapon.

34

As I cautiously move in on him, I smell chicken. I pull out my gun and my flashlight. I say, "All right, you. Get outta there." I shine my flashlight on him.

Who the hell d'you think it is? It's my father. He has a big bag of chicken cacciatore and bread, and half a bottle of wine and a napkin.

He smiles at me and he says in Italian, "My son, you must be hungry."

I say, "What the hell are you doing here? Will you get outta here! What are you following me for?"

He says, "No, no, I no follow you. I know you hungry." He insists I eat something. I'm very embarrassed that somebody's going to see me, but he sets everything up in this hallway. I'll never forget this. He has a box there and he puts the white napkin on the box and he puts the food out on it, all neat, and I eat the chicken and the Italian bread and half a glass of wine.

He cleans everything up, gives me a big kiss and goes home. Other nights, I sense a shadow following me and I know who it is. He's following me while I'm on patrol. I chase him and he runs away. How can anybody go wrong with a dad like that?

My dad becomes a well-known figure in the 32nd Precinct. All the other patrolmen know him by sight. The guys in the radio cars, they shout out to him, "Hi, there, Mr. Schiano!"

The guys on patrol all salute him. And he brings food to the guys working in the clerical room inside the stationhouse. He knows them all, everything about them, because of me.

Once, in the subway, he sees a young patrolman trying to cool off a drunken Irishman. The drunk jumps the cop and knocks his uniform hat off. When my father sees the cap fall to the ground, he goes wild. He jumps on the drunk and bites his ear. Now the drunk starts beating my dad and the patrol-

35

man . . . he's some handful. My dad grabs the cop's nightstick and smacks it over the drunk's head. He goes down, unconscious.

This happens in the 32nd Precinct. The cops arrive and the drunk and the patrolman and my dad are taken to Harlem Hospital. I'm riding in a patrol car with a patrolman named Eddie Egan—later I work with him and Sonny Grosso at the end of the "French Connection" case—when a radio message comes over for us to respond to Harlem Hospital. I say, "10–4" and we go to the emergency room.

There's a whole mess of cops in there and who do I see sitting down and being treated by a doctor but my dad. I go berserk. I say, "What the hell happened to you?" My dad has already told the other patrolmen what my reaction would be, that I'd be mad and would they please defend him.

Some of the old-time patrolmen say, "Quiet, Anthony, quiet! Don't talk to your father like that. He came to the assistance of a patrolman on the subway."

I look at the patrolman and he says, "Yeah, he did." They all pat my dad on the back and there's a sergeant there and he says, "Okay, Anthony, go on, take your father home." I put him in the patrol car and, boy, am I mad at him. I say, "You can't do this. You can't hang around the precinct and follow me. I'm a big man now. I've been in Korea and I'm a cop. You can't come on patrols with me—I won't stand for it."

He smiles at me and he says, "You may be big now, but you're still my little boy." What can I do? I take him home.

Walking my post, I learn about people —the good ones, the crazy ones, the funny ones, the pathetic ones and the bad ones. I learn about the incidents which give all cops the horrors—family fights. I learn to stay away from them if at

36

all possible. I learn that if you have to get involved, you never take sides. I learn that family fights always end with the family uniting and turning on the cop.

Drunks, they're almost as bad. They'll drape themselves over you lovingly and then they'll throw up all over your uniform. But you're supposed to keep your post clean of drunks and hoboes, so you have to do something about them. One bad spot on my post for drunks is a post office on 138th Street where they congregate. There's a particular guy always there, and this one time I call an ambulance to take him to a hospital. In the ambulance, he vomits all over me and when we get to the hospital, I have to hang around for hours in my filthy, vile-smiling uniform while they take care of the red tape.

A couple of nights later, I see this same guy collapsed on a stoop near Fifth Avenue. Oh, I think, not again! I look around to make sure there's nobody in sight. I half pick him up and I drag him across Fifth Avenue and I sit him down very comfortably on a bench which happens to be in the 25th Precinct. He looks at me affectionately and settles back into slumberland.

Nearby, there's a public telephone. I go and phone the 25th Precinct and, like a good citizen, report there's a man sleeping on a bench who needs medical attention. I put the phone down, slip into a doorway and watch.

In a little while, a radio car pulls up at the bench. Two patrolmen get out and go over to the drunk. They give him a tap and he doesn't stir. They look up and down the street and then they pick him up and drag him back across Fifth Avenue onto my post. The lousy bastards. They drive off.

I go over to the drunk and shake him. "Hey, Mac," I say, "get up and move off." He just smiles at me and closes his eyes. Again I drag him over Fifth Avenue to the bench and again I telephone the 25th Precinct.

"Hey," I say, "that guy on the park bench is back there. I think you'd better send an ambulance."

Instead of an ambulance, the same radio car shows up. Sure enough, they drag him back to my post. But this time, just as they're putting him down, he heaves up all over them, splashing them with his vomit. They swear, get back in their car and zoom off. I hope they stink in their car.

Now that I know the drunk has heaved, I'm more comfortable. I'm pretty sure he's vomited everything he's got, so I call an ambulance and haul him off to Harlem Hospital.

Walking a post at night is a great time for thinking and for recalling the past, good and bad. From a respectable point of view, I guess most of my past is bad.

As a kid, I grew up on East 114th Street and to the end of my teens that was my turf. What I remember most of all was the constant fighting between my mom and dad. They just didn't get along and when I was nine years old, they separated. I lived mostly with my mom, but sometimes I moved in for a while with my dad.

The neighborhood was no bargain . . . tenements and crummy streets and lots of people out of work. In those days, they'd laugh you off the block if you told them that one day it would be called Spanish Harlem. It was as Italian as Naples, just as poverty-stricken and just as clannish.

The cops were mostly Irish, but the real law came from the Big Gees, the big gangsters, the men in silk suits who had expensive cars and never lifted a finger in honest work. They ran the gambling and the narcotics that were beginning to show up.

My mom, she was born in New York but Dad came from Italy by way of Galveston, Texas, where he jumped ship.

He never made much money. He survived by painting the tenements and, sometimes, the Mob-owned bars and restaurants in the neighborhood. That's how he got to know people like Joe Valachi.

Sometimes he stole milk from doorsteps so that I could grow up strong and healthy. He looked for apartments which had more than one milk bottle outside the door.

"Anthony," he used to say, "I never take when there's only one bottle. I think, well, maybe they need that one bottle. But if there's two or three, then I take one and leave them some."

On East 114th Street, we had a bopping gang, the Italian Dukes. I still have the gang shirt up in my attic at home . . . black satin with a green map of Italy on the front. On the back, it says, "Italian Dukes." If you weren't a member of a gang, you were nothing.

The Dukes, we kept the blacks and the Puerto Ricans off our turf. If they came east of Third Avenue, they were in trouble. If we went west of Third Avenue . . . say, into the 32nd Precinct . . . we were in trouble.

In the Dukes, we had guys like Bo, built like a refrigerator, who'd do anything to get a laugh. Always in trouble in school. He'd harass the teachers, goose the girls, do anything so long as he got a laugh from it. He was the first guy to break a window, to throw a rock at a car. He was very short and I guess he was always trying to prove himself.

Another was Tony Cimo. His brother was in the Mob. This brother, he ended up with two bullets in the back of his head and a canary stuck in his mouth. I guess they did that to him because he'd been singing in the wrong places.

Jimmy Nocita. All his brothers, his father and his mother went to jail at one time or another. Yeah, his mother, too. There was Gene Lanza, the thinker, who acted as war counselor for the Italian Dukes. He planned the street fighting. And there was Kid Rae . . . Kid Rae who always carried a .22 caliber zip gun, a knife and a lead pipe in the back of his waistband.

He was a real psycho. "One day," he used to say, "I'll kill a nigger or a spic. I tell ya I've gotta do it."

There was a mean, retarded kid named Zero. He had a cock you wouldn't believe. It was so long, he could beat you to death with it. He used to go downtown to entertain homos with it to make money for the Italian Dukes.

There was One-eyed Nancy (a great body but a lousy face) who put on exhibitions with Zero to make money for the gang.

One evening, we're all planning to go to a movie around Times Square. Kid Rae tells me, "I gotta get some money. I'll be right back."

"Where are ya going?" I ask.

"Come on, then," he says. "Take a walk with me."

We go around the corner and walk up the stairs to the roof of his building, where we wait. This is the roof where we do our necking. I see a dark figure approaching from another roof. As he gets closer, I recognize him as a guy we used to play ball with at school. I know he's a junkie.

He gives Kid Rae some money and Kid Rae hands over something to him. I know what it has to be . . . junk.

Kid Rae won't talk about it. I know a couple of other kids around the neighborhood are also selling stuff. We go down and join the rest of the gang. Bo has stolen a vegetable truck to take us downtown to the movies. He's so short he can hardly see over the steering wheel. Off we go.

We get as far as the East 90s when the truck stalls. We can't get it going again, so we pile out. We start walking, pushing over garbage cans as we go and jostling pedestrians.

40

Suddenly, we hear the screech of tires and the slamming of doors. Three cops come out of their radio car and run at us, their nightsticks out.

"Okay, wise guys," one of them says, "get up against the wall." They push us into a hallway and as we go, I can hear the clatter of metal as Kid Rae gets rid of his zip gun, knife and pipe. The cops know what's going on. They tell Kid Rae they saw him throw away his weapons. He just smiles and says nothing. They look at us, disgusted. Finally, they kick us in the ass and tell us to get off the street.

The worst were the fights with the blacks and Puerto Ricans. They scared me shitless. One came about because I was trying to get the Dukes to come with me to the Boys Club of New York on East 111th Street. Finally, they agree to come with me to a basketball game between kids from the neighborhood and some blacks from Lenox Hill.

All the Italian Dukes come and we go up to the balcony. The home team comes out and everybody claps. Then the black team comes out and everybody claps except for the Dukes, who boo. The game's rough, a couple of the blacks giving the elbow to the whites and the whites doing the same thing. There are fouls and whistles blowing and penalties and the black team wins. My gang won't stand for that.

We go down to the locker room and Kid Rae, the psycho, says to one big black kid, "You niggers won 'cause you cheated. Fuck you." Well, that's it.

Gene Lanza says to go outside and wait for them. We see one of the black guys go to the telephone and we know a rumble's coming up. Gene sends a Duke back to our clubhouse to get our stash and he comes back with a large burlap bag. Inside are our zip guns, chains and pipes. Kid Rae doesn't need anything—he's always armed.

The zip guns are handed out and we line up facing the

doors, waiting for the blacks to come out. The zip guns are made from car aerials which are just right for .22 caliber cartridges. They'd penetrate a tin door. We tried it.

Someone comes out and says the black kids are getting ready for us. I get a feeling in my stomach. We all pull out our zip guns. We pull back the springs to load them. Some of us have got baseball bats and chains as well.

I say to myself, "I'm crazy. I'm gonna get myself killed." But I can't leave now. I gotta prove I'm part of them.

Kid Rae doesn't take out his .22. He takes out his black-jack. He's very quiet. Jimmy Nocita, a tough guy with his hands, he goes next to Kid Rae and he yells at the blacks, "All right, motherfuckers, come on out. Come on, niggers."

A black comes to the door and says, "Hey, man, what've we done? We ain't done nothing to you." The black guys are trying to stall for time. They're waiting.

The team coaches come out and tell us to go home. They say it's poor sportsmanship. One of the Dukes gives them a razz. They see trouble.

All of a sudden, up the street from west to east we see a truck coming right for us. Out pile about twenty blacks. When we see this, we start to run for First Avenue, firing back as we go, hiding behind ashcans and in doorways.

But Kid stays where he is. "Kid," we scream, "come on, let's go." He just smiles. He's got his eye on one of the blacks coming out of the club. He goes for him. He grabs him by the throat. The black guy doesn't even defend himself . . . he doesn't believe it. Kid Rae brings up his blackjack and bashes him right in the face.

Then he fights his way out of the blacks around him and he runs after us. We run across First Avenue to Thomas

42

Jefferson Park, the black guys chasing us. I don't fire my gun. I'm so frightened, shaking in my boots. Kid Rae and Jimmy Nocita and the others are swinging with their bats.

I pick up a club and I hit this black guy across the chest. He screams and runs and I go for another black who's beating up on Zero. From behind, more blacks are bashing me. I think, "My God, I'm going to get killed."

I see a bright red light and, Jesus, I feel pain. I fall. I grab my face. My hands are full of blood. The Dukes manage to carry me out of the park and they get me to Polytechnic Hospital. The doctors sew me up with six stitches.

When I get out of the hospital, all bandaged up, I head back to the clubhouse on 114th Street.

I see more blacks waiting there. They know where we're from. Zero shows up and when he sees all the blacks, he climbs a lampost. Nobody sees him except me and Bo. We run into a building and climb up to a rooftop and from the roof we look down.

We see the blacks smashing windows, firing their zip guns, busting into cars, breaking car aerials, turning over garbage cans, all the time screaming and yelling.

Finally, the cops arrive, about seven radio cars. They chase off the black guys and the Italian Dukes begin to straggle back, some bleeding, most with ripped clothes. Somebody shouts up to Zero on top of the lamppost, "Okay, Zero, it's all over . . . come on down."

He looks down at us and he says, "Fuck you. I'm not coming down yet." But he does.

One day, when I was eighteen, I was at Times Square in the subway when I saw a sign, "Join the Army." I was disgusted with everything. I hadn't done well at school.

I knew I had to break away from the guys in the neighbor-

43

hood or I'd be going their way, running for the racketeers. I knew enough about the street to do it.

The recruiting sergeant in the army booth said I could allot money to my mother while in the service. I signed up. The first few months at Fort Dix, I made friends and even got invited to their homes. That was something else, to see a good home where all the family sat down to dinner together. I never had that and that's what I wanted. But, in spite of army training, I was still a wise guy, the kid from East 114th Street.

I caught pneumonia and I was taken to the hospital at Fort Dix for more than two months. While I was recovering, the doctor gave me permission to go on a weekend pass, but the corporal in charge of the ward, a rebel from the South, said I couldn't go. He didn't like Yankees, especially a Guinea Yankee.

With another patient in the ward, a red-haired Puerto Rican from 104th Street, I decide to take off. The Puerto Rican wants to go because he has a problem. His wife is having an affair with his best friend. He wants to solve the problem by killing his best friend.

We get out through a window in the ward and head for Manhattan, where we separate.

From a drugstore near home, I phone my father. "Listen," I say, "I'm in New York. I got a pass from the hospital."

"You what?" He sounds suspicious.

"I got a pass. I'm gonna have a meal with Momma and then I'll be over."

"No," he says. "You come right over here now. Bring your mother over and we'll have dinner here."

I go to my mom's place and I dress up in a freshly pressed uniform and then I go to my dad's place. He starts questioning me. I manage to get away from him. I tell him I want to go and see some of my pals in the neighborhood. At First Avenue and 118th Street, I run into some girls I know. They gather around me and we talk. They compliment me on how smart I look in my uniform. I like that. I'm kidding them and telling them about army life and doing a bit of flirting when a truck pulls up to the curb.

Two men get out and before I know it, one of them has his arm around my neck and the other twists my left arm up behind my back. They're M.P.s. They search me, while the girls look on, and then they toss me into the truck and speed off.

My dad has called them because he doesn't believe I have a pass.

The M.P.s take me to the stationhouse where they're based at that time . . . the 32nd Precinct, the same one where later I start out as a cop. So, the first time I ever entered that stationhouse I was in handcuffs and I was under arrest. The whole stupid affair ended with me being busted down from Pfc. and being sent back to duty.

Before I'm shipped to Korea, I get some leave—this time official. I go back to East Harlem and see the guys. They haven't changed. One day, we go to Orchard Beach, me very sharp in my uniform, them in casual clothes. We see two girls lying on a blanket and we go over and plop down on the blanket with them. One of the guys says, "You don't mind, d'you?" as if they had any choice. This one girl, she says, "I'll tell you what, you just keep the blanket." And she gets up and walks away.

I go after her to try and talk to her but she calls me a hoodlum. I'm persistent, however, and she warms up a bit. Finally she lets me take her home. Her name is Helen. When

I ask her for a date, she says that first I've got to meet her parents. That's not the way it is on East 114th.

I fight it, but eventually I say okay. I meet her mother and father, who live in the Bronx. Her father is a large man. He's also a New York cop. He's Italian but he doesn't like me because I come from East Harlem and he knows what kids who come from East Harlem are like.

Her mother, though, she likes me. She's a great cook and every time I show up at their apartment, she has a spread laid out . . . cold cuts, delicacies, coffee and sodas. Helen and I, we date every day of my leave. We go for walks and to the movies, holding hands, real kid stuff. If the guys from East Harlem had seen us . . . But then I have to go overseas.

When I come back, we dock at Brooklyn and I'm one of the last off the ship. I watch other GIs being greeted and I feel a little envious because I don't think anybody from my family will be there. I'm feeling sorry for myself.

I'm looking over the rail when, suddenly, I hear a young kid crying, "An-thon-ee . . . An-thon-ee!" I stare and there are my two little cousins waving at me. With them are my mother and my aunts. I get off that ship fast. I run to my mother and then as I'm holding her, who do I see but my dad. They'd got together again, just to give me a good welcome home.

My dad tells me a girl called Ellen telephoned him and said I'm coming home. Of course, it was Helen. She told him she'd seen a newspaper clipping listing GIs from the metropolitan area who were returning and my name was on the list. He invited her to come with him to meet me but she said no—it should be just the family.

My dad went and collected my mom and my aunts and he took a taxi and they all came out to meet me. For a moment there, when I see him with Mom, I get the feeling that maybe they're together again, maybe everything's changed and I can have the kind of family life I want. But I find out, no, it's just for this special occasion.

Even so, we go back to the city and my dad cooks us a big feast at his place . . . he's cooked for himself for years and he's good at it. Immediately after, I go to see Helen in the Bronx and we go up on the roof of her building and we talk. I know this is the girl for me.

Soon after, I buy my first car, a Chevy Bel-Air, a real clunker, and I drive round to take Helen out. Her dad still doesn't like me, but her mom whispers to him, "Shush, Henry, he's a good boy." But he's suspicious of me and my car. He tells his son to sneak downstairs and take the number of my license plate so that he, as a cop, can check it out.

Helen hasn't met my friends, the Italian Dukes, except for that time on the beach when she called us hoodlums. I decide it's time she met them, and it's arranged that I take her out in my car to have pizza and drinks with them in a bar on 76th Street. They've got a couple of cars and some girls.

My girl's dressed up and so am I because it's a Saturday night but the bar's a bucket of blood, a real crummy joint, and their girls are in sloppy clothes, shirts and dirty pants. We have a heartburn dinner and some drinks, but Helen will only have a Coke. The other girls decide they don't like her. To them, she's a snob.

They ask her which gang she belongs to and she says, "I don't belong to a gang." She doesn't know what they're talking about.

They ask her how many boy friends she's got. She says, "I've only got one." They laugh and they make jokes about her. The Dukes get me in a corner and say they don't like her . . . they say I should ditch her. One of 'em says, "You can't bring her around. She's a drag." And, you know, they have me believing them. Here, I think I'm so smart and yet they have me fooled.

We all leave the bar and the Dukes decide to drag race up the East River to 116th Street, the loser to buy the beer when we get there. That's too much for Helen. "I thought you'd changed," she says. "You haven't. You're a hoodlum, just like they are. Let me off and I'll take a train home."

By now, we're on the East Side Drive, so I keep on going past the 116th Street exit heading for her home in the Bronx. On the way I get a little cocky. "We don't like snobs," I say. "That's what you are, a snob." She doesn't say anything and when we get to her place, she gets out very quietly.

I'm driving away, going home, and I have to stop for a red light and as I'm waiting there, I suddenly say to myself, "What the hell are you doing? What are you, crazy?"

I drive round the block back to her home. I run up the stairs, ring her doorbell. Her mom comes and says, "What is it, Tony?" She knows something's wrong.

"Can I speak to Helen?"

"Sure, come on in."

"If you don't mind, I'd like to see her out here." She goes inside and in a few minutes, Helen comes, her eyes all red like she's been crying. She's wiping her nose with a hankie.

I'm standing looking at her. Then I throw my arms around her and I kiss her. "I'm going to marry you," I say. Some months later, we agree we'll get engaged but I don't get off the hook that easy. I tell her I love her and want to marry her. But I have to do it by the book. She says I have to get on one knee and ask, "May I have your hand in marriage?"

I'm against it, but, dammit, she makes me do it and when I propose like that, she says yes.

48

Helen's mom makes drapes for the apartment we're going to live in, up in the Bronx, and she prepares her wedding gown. When we walk down the aisle at St. Anthony's Church, my dad and my mom burst out into tears.

By this time, I'm a cop and I've invited some brother officers from the 32nd Precinct and they congratulate me. No Italian Dukes, though. I'm through with them now.

3

IT's not easy being an Italian patrolman in a police department that's bossed by the Irish. The Irish, they've been running the cops for years . . . they think the department belongs to them.

At the 32nd Precinct, I had one big, fat Irish sergeant who tried to give me a hard time. One day, I'm on the street and he drives up in a police car. I give him a snappy salute and the car stops.

"Hey, Guinea," he shouts, "come here." I don't move.

"Guinea, I'm calling you," he says.

"Are you talking to me, sergeant?" I say, very polite.

"Yes, Guinea, I'm talking to you," he says. I think he's a bit drunk.

"Please don't call me a Guinea, sergeant," I say. "I don't answer when I'm called that."

"Fuck you," he says. "You're off post. Why?"

I tell him I'm standing in for a patrolman on an adjoining post who's gone for dinner. It's all according to the rules.

I'm right and he knows it. "Listen, Guinea," he says. "When I tell you to do something, you do it." And off he drives.

I try not to let that sort of thing bother me. Instead, I

concentrate on my work. I make my first worthwhile arrest. It comes after I've finished a 4 P.M. to midnight tour. I've changed my clothes and I'm driving home along Eighth Avenue, still in Harlem, when I see a bunch of black guys fighting.

As I stop and get out of my car, I see one of them has a gun in his hand. He's facing another guy who's trying to shield himself with a trash can cover. Standing behind my car with my revolver drawn, I shout, "Drop the gun . . . I'm a police officer."

The fellow with the gun turns towards me and, as he does that, the other guy uses the trash can cover to hit him on the head. Bop! Down goes the guy with the gun. It turns out to be a pellet gun, but it looks very realistic. I lock up the whole group. I make other arrests. For narcotics, robbery, purse snatching. Some departmental recognitions come my way. The detectives begin to notice me because of my arrests. At this time, detectives, not patrolmen, handled processing, such as fingerprinting.

After my tours, I used to ask detectives if they would take me out on patrol in my own time. They liked my aggressiveness, my interest in the way they worked. Two black detectives, Jones and Reel, they let me go out with them and they let me make some of the arrests. I was impressed with the respect they got on the street. When they grabbed a suspect, he always called them "Mr. Jones" and "Mr. Reel."

There were three patrolmen and a sergeant in the 10th Division, known as "The Four Horsemen." Only the sergeant was white. They were something. They patrolled in an unmarked car and they responded only to robberies, bar fights, riots or a cop in trouble. They were big guys and they specialized in dealing with bar fights, where everything goes.

They agreed to take me out on patrol and I learned from them.

They told me there was only one way to stop a bar fight, like the time at the Lotus Bar on Lenox Avenue. We respond to a call there and the Four Horsemen pile out of the car. They go into that bar like a human tank.

They smash their way right to the back, devastating furniture, bottles, and humans as they go. Then they turn and, shoulder to shoulder, do the same thing going out. When they're finished, the fight is over and there's not much left of the bar . . . just broken chairs and tables and groaning customers. It's the only way to handle a bar fight because once a bar fight starts, everybody goes mad. The Four Horsemen never use their guns . . . just their nightsticks and muscle.

On my post, there are gentler times. I'm on a school crossing one time when I get word that a woman is sick in a nearby tenement. I go up there and find a pregnant girl dressed in a kimono. Her mother is with her and she says the pains are coming very close together, so I go and telephone for an ambulance. When I come back, I remember lessons in the Police Academy where we were told to try to make expectant mothers comfortable until help arrives.

I walk the girl to her bed. As she lifts her leg to get between the sheets, I hear a thud. I look down and, oh, my God, there's a baby lying there, squirming in a mass of blood. I feel a bit funny, but I take her kimono and wrap the baby in it and place it beside the mother on the bed.

I have to sit down. There's a knock on the door and in come a couple of cops with an ambulance attendant.

They look at me and the attendant says, "What's the matter, officer. Are you sick?" I just shake my head and point to the baby. They do what's necessary and take the mother and child off to the hospital.

The girl's mother insists I stay and have a cup of coffee and, to tell the truth, I need it. When I leave, she gives me a kiss.

One night tour, I call in to the stationhouse at the required time and a sergeant comes on. "Patrolman Schiano, Post 35, sarge," I say.

"Yeah," he says. "Listen, I want you to relieve Patrolman Divot. Go to 30 West 133rd Street, apartment 2B. There's a DOA up there. Wait for the morgue wagon and get the name of the driver. Okay?"

Off I go. I'm a bit uneasy because this is my first experience as a cop with a dead person. Divot lets me in. The first thing I notice is that the apartment smells to high heaven.

"I'm here to relieve you," I say to the patrolman. He's already putting on his coat and hat. "Have fun," he says, and the next minute he's gone. Now I'm alone and I don't like it. There's not much light, just a bulb in the kitchen which gives an eerie yellow glow. I can see dirty dishes in the sink. The place is pretty filthy.

After a few minutes, I sit down and thumb through my memo book. Then I think I'd better take a look at the body.

I go into one bedroom, expecting to find the body there. There's no light so I pull out my flashlight and shine it around. The room has trunks and cases and clothes but no body. It has to be in the other bedroom.

But the door to the second bedroom is closed and at first when I push it, it won't budge. Finally, I give a good shove and it opens. The electric light doesn't work in here either.

Using my flashlight, I check out the bed, but there's no body in it. To the left, there's a night table with a radio and

53

medicines but, again, no body. To the right, there's a dresser and a mirror. When I shine my light in that direction, the mirror throws back the beams full in my face. I'm getting a bit edgy. Still there's no body.

I go deeper into the room and behind me the door starts to close. I swing around and, oh, my God, there he is.

The dead man is hanging on the back of the door. An electric cord goes from his neck up to a nail. A suicide. He's been there for three days. He's a thin black man, but his face is all bloated from death. His tongue's hanging out. The man is literally blue in the face. The cord is buried in his blue-black flesh. His eyes are staring. I get out of there fast, closing the door carefully behind me. I go and wait in the kitchen. I'm sweating.

A bit later, the morgue men show up. I tell them the body is in the bedroom.

One of them says, "Okay, officer, we'll take care of it. You can go now."

I want to go but I say, "I can't. I've got to stay here until the body's gone."

They go into the bedroom, carrying a body-bag, a large leather container with a zipper. They close the door. I can hear them getting the body down from the door. I can hear other things. There's the sound of furniture being moved around and the sound of ripping. They're in there about twenty minutes.

After they come out with the filled body-bag and leave, I'm curious about what's been going on in there. I go in and take a peek. It's as though a tornado has hit the room. The mattress is slashed. All the drawers are pulled out. Clothes are strewn all over the place, pockets turned inside out. The bed is in a different position.

54

I report it but I don't find out what happens, if anything. There were other bodies. A cop's career is littered with bodies. One time, I'm doing a midnight to 8 A.M. tour on 145th Street between Seventh and Eighth Avenues. Two older black patrolmen are on the adjoining posts and they're keeping an eye open for me because they know I'm a rookie. We hear screaming coming from the middle of my block, and we all run there. A woman tells us there's been a fight on the roof. She says there are three men up there.

When we get to the roof, everybody's gone. But we hear a noise down in the yard at the back, a sort of mumbling, shuffling noise. We go down and find a guy lying there with a broken neck. He's been thrown off the roof. He hits two fire escapes on the way down and he's a godawful mess. He lives a short time but when we get him to a hospital, he's dead.

He and the other guys were junkies. They threw him off the roof because he screwed them on a junk deal.

While I'm a patrolman in the 32nd Precinct, I start getting a reputation for being aggressive. I come in with a lot of narcotics arrests. I look so young, the dope pushers don't take me seriously at first, so they aren't afraid of me.

I start to develop informers. The only good cop is a cop who has good informers. I get informers by doing favors for them, helping them if they're in trouble or giving them a dollar or two.

I go for a few dollars out of my own pocket and I'm not earning much as a patrolman. It's worth it.

As I develop informers on the street, my arrests soar. I get word there's a guy selling grass in a luncheonette in upper Harlem, on the west side of Seventh Avenue. But there's trouble coming up in the person of my commander, Captain Stone, who's replaced Captain Sampson.

55

He's a stout, flabby guy, no muscle. He doesn't want any waves in his precinct. This night, he comes behind the desk before we turn out, to give us instructions. He talks about traffic and gambling.

Then he says, "I don't want anybody to make any narcotics arrests. I don't want my men to get involved in that. We have narcotics detectives to do that." Am I pissed off. I've got this tip about the luncheonette and I'm gonna make an arrest and this captain tells me not to. I'm definitely displeased. The hell with him, I'm gonna make the arrest.

I go off and see my informer and he tells me the grass pusher is sitting at the far end of the counter of this luncheonette. I go to the luncheonette and I take off my cap and I peek through a corner of the window. There's some customers sitting in there and at the far end of the counter is a shaven-headed black, drinking coffee and smoking a cigarette while he's talking to the waitress. He's a big sonofabitch with very white teeth and purple gums.

I put my hat back on and I take a deep breath and I go into the luncheonette. Everything goes quiet. I'm watching this guy's hands—you never watch a man's eyes, you watch his hands. It's something out of a cowboy movie when the swinging doors open and the sheriff comes through. Except for one thing . . . I'm scared shitless.

I move over to him and as I get near, his right hand, which is on the other side of him from me, goes to his inner breast pocket. This is where the informer says he keeps his grass. I throw him a bear hug. He's surprised . . . he's bigger than me but I'm stronger. But now I can't get the cuffs on him. I'm just hugging him.

I have to throw him off. I suck up mucus from my nose and throat and I spit the oyster out, right in his face. Now

56

he's even more surprised and in that moment I twist his arms to his back and handcuff him. I reach in his pocket and pull out the packet of pot.

During this, my hat falls to the ground and gets sawdust on it. I pick it up and put it back on, but now the customers are muttering because a white man is taking one of their own. I say, "Nobody get excited. Everybody keep their seats. Everything's okay. We're going to the 32nd Precinct."

I slowly move out, with him in front of me. I'm holding his collar . . . I have to reach up a bit because he's taller than me. Outside, I look around for help, a radio car or a patrolman, because it'd be very dangerous for me to walk through Harlem, a white cop taking in a black like that. I need transportation bad and this guy knows I'm looking around and he knows I'm uncomfortable because the people from the luncheonette come out still grumbling and form a semicircle around us.

There are no cops around. I walk him out to the middle of the street and start walking behind him down the yellow line. My hand is still on his collar but, suddenly, he breaks. He ducks into a building with me maybe five yards behind him. He's fast and I'm clumsy with my heavy clothes and my belt and gun and memo book and flashlight. He goes through the hallway and down the stairs to an alleyway.

I stop. It's dark and I can't hear him. I don't turn on my flashlight because I don't want him to be able to see me coming. Instead I pull my gun out and start down the stairway. They're very rickety. By now, I'm sure he's got his hands in front of him. If you know what you're doing, you can get your hands from back to your front even with cuffs on.

The stairs start to sway under me and I'm just about

halfway down when the whole goddam stairs collapse under me. I crash down with them, and as I'm falling, I hear a grunt. The stairs and me, we've collapsed onto the guy.

My gun goes skittering across the ground and I suffer some minor injuries. I crawl over, retrieve my gun and then I pull this guy, moaning and groaning, from under the stairs. When we get back to the street, bruised and dirty, I find a radio car there. Somebody's called the cops.

I've hurt my ankle and my back and when I get back to the stationhouse, a buddy takes over the job of processing the prisoner. You wouldn't believe the paperwork in a simple arrest. I go to Harlem Hospital for treatment and then I come back to the stationhouse.

Anytime a patrolman is hurt like I was, his commanding officer has to be notified and he has to interview the patrolman. So this Captain Stone is told about me and he has to come in from his home to see me. He has me stand in front of his desk, no emotion on his face. But I know what he's thinking . . . it's 3 A.M. now and he's been dragged from his warm bed because of me.

He looks at me and finally he says, "Patrolman Schiano, what happened?" I tell him about the arrest and the chase and the fall down the rickety old stairs. When I've finished, he stands up behind his desk and he starts to scream.

"Didn't I tell you not to take any action involving narcotics? Didn't I tell you to stay away from that sort of thing?"

"But, captain," I start to say, "I got this information."

"I don't care what information you got. Don't you try to explain to me. You disobeyed my instructions, Schiano."

"But, sir . . ."

"I'm making a report on the blotter that you were not injured in the line of duty. That will be the official report. Now get outta here."

58

I know what that means. It means I can't claim for sickness or if, God forbid, I'm maimed, I can't get any compensation. My ankle is real swollen now and I hobble out. I don't go sick because I wouldn't be paid for it and I can't afford that. More than that, he takes me off my patrol post and assigns me to St. Nicholas Park. With the squirrels. For three months, I play with the squirrels.

I don't make arrests. I can't. I try so hard but I can't.

But I still have friends. Some of the sergeants and lieutenants, they know I did right on that arrest and when Captain Stone is away or off duty, they call me in to do clerical duty in the stationhouse. That gives me a chance to make arrests.

While I'm working in the stationhouse, I listen to the police radio and every time there's a crime being committed nearby, like a block away, I dash out of the stationhouse and head for the scene. I'm just in my shirt and pants and wearing my small gun.

You're not supposed to go outside unless you have your full uniform on and you're carrying your service revolver. They used to yell at me, "Schiano, where're you going? Come back." But I'd keep going, and I'd make an arrest, whether it was for assault or larceny or a bullshit robbery. I'd waltz in with the arrest before the patrol car could even get to the scene.

One time, a lieutenant, Jack Lake, thirty years on the job, puts me on the telephone switchboard. He likes me and he knows this Captain Stone is after my ass. A call comes in that an assault is being committed in a hallway about a block from the precinct house.

I jump up and he screams at me, "Don't you dare, Schiano!"

I say, "It's all right, lieutenant, I'm just going out for lunch."

59

"No," he says, "I don't want you to have lunch now. You stay right here."

"But, lieutenant," I say, "I just want to get me a sandwich." I run right out and instead of coming back with a sandwich, I come back with a prisoner who's been beating up a woman halfway up the block. It's a big laugh, but it means more arrests for me.

Then, lo and behold, Stone is transferred and we get another commander, Captain James Forth. He comes in like a clean, country breeze. He wants arrests. He wants to clean up the precinct. He starts looking for aggressive patrolmen for high-crime posts. Some guys want to do clerical duty, to get off the streets, but not me. I want arrests. Captain Forth interviews his sergeants to find out which are the active patrolmen. They give him my name.

Beautiful. I'm put back on street post and then I'm assigned to a radio car which is very busy. I start making arrest after arrest, but I'm so busy, I'm not giving out many summonses for traffic violations.

One night, a sergeant calls me in and he looks at my summons book and he sees I haven't given one for a month. I tell him that's because I'm too busy making arrests for misdemeanors and felonies.

"Bullshit!" he says. "Don't tell me that. I'm giving you a complaint." That's bad. It means if you're found guilty, you can have pay deducted. But for me it's worse because I want to be interviewed for detective and I don't want anything on my record. The sergeant says he's going to send me in to be questioned by Captain Forth about my low summons quota.

"Patrolman Schiano reporting as directed," I say, saluting the captain.

"Hi, there, Schiano," he says. "I understand you've got a

little problem. Why don't you tell me what it's all about?"
I tell him I've been so busy making arrests I haven't had time
to issue summonses.

He's got a little gray index box on a side table and he opens
it and looks at the cards which show how many arrests each
patrolman has made for the month. He looks at my card and
it's completely filled.

Then he looks at me and says, "I know you, Schiano. You
were assigned to St. Nicholas Park because you made a
narcotics arrest, weren't you? You fell on top of the pusher,
didn't you?"

"Yes, sir."

"Okay, kid," he says, "listen to me. You don't give out
summonses. You make arrests instead. Got it?"

"Yes, sir!"

He dismisses me and tells me to send in the sergeant.
Naturally, I hang around the doorway and I hear the captain
tell the sergeant, "Instead of looking for summonses, look for
men who make arrests and clean up this precinct." He
sounds very cold. "In the meantime, leave Schiano alone."

Wow! I could've pissed in my pants. After that, I do even
better on making arrests.

Later, I get a transfer, to fly police helicopters for the
aviation section. I'd got a commercial flying license at the
end of 1956. I love to fly.

I didn't do too well. Flying helicopters is a helluva lot
different to fixed-wing planes. All the helicopter pilots were
German, with a couple of Irish, and they didn't have much
time for an Italian. I couldn't seem to get the hang of the
damned copters.

My instructor was an acting sergeant called Erhardt.
Nowadays, there's no such rank but there was then. He got

this rank, without a civil service test, because of his fantastic ability to fly and his experience in aviation. But, basically, he was a patrolman. He looked like a real German, blond straight hair and blue eyes. He was always in the newspapers because he was always rescuing people off smokestacks, that sort of thing. He was the only guy who could do something like that.

But he had no patience with me. He didn't like me, that was easy to see. When he tried to instruct me, I had difficulty with this Bell helicopter and as the months went by, I still couldn't handle the damn thing.

My dad, he knew I was flying around up there in the helicopters. We used to patrol over Brooklyn, the West Side Highway, the George Washington Bridge, lower Manhattan, the Queensboro, the upper Bronx and down south to the East River Drive.

He was working at a factory on the East River Drive and he fixed it so he was painting a water tower, 200–300 feet above the ground. This summer day, I'm flying with another pilot.

I ask him if we can fly near this water tower, Of course, it would cost me later on—I'd have to buy him lunch, but it's worth it. He agrees.

As we approach the tower, there I can see my father. He's waving his hands at me. All covered with paint. As we get close, he waves even harder and he throws a kiss at me. I do this a number of times. Just like at the precinct, he gets so that he knows every helicopter and if I'm in it.

After a year, this acting sergeant recommends that I be transferred out of the aviation section because I'm not good enough for it. They send me back to the 32nd Precinct, which is where I belong, I suppose.

When I get this transfer, it's one of the biggest heartbreaks

I ever have. I want to be a pilot and now it's all shattered.

But the day before I'm to be transferred from Floyd Bennett Field, I'm on patrol with three or four other helicopters to escort a boat called the *Mayflower,* a replica of the one the Pilgrims came over in from England, down the Hudson River.

We go on station, right over the *Mayflower,* which is carrying a bunch of dignitaries, including Mayor Wagner and the police commissioner of that time—I think it was Steve Kennedy. Now, the helicopters are so low that our down-draft sucks out the wind from the ship's sails. It goes out of control and starts floundering sideways.

Everybody on the deck, Wagner and the commissioner among them, looks up and starts shaking their fists at us. Finally, they get control of the boat—I think a tugboat got a line aboard and we get ordered back to Floyd Bennett.

The next day when I go back to the 32nd Precinct as a result of Erhardt's recommendation, the story goes around that I'm dumped from the aviation section because I deflated the *Mayflower's* sails.

It's a big joke. It goes all around the department and up to this day, my name is always connected with two things—my undercover work and the day I got transferred because I screwed up the voyage of the *Mayflower.*

You should have seen my father's face when I tell him I'm being transferred back to patrol duty. He knows it's because this guy Erhardt wants me out of the aviation section. I never saw a man hate so much. The things he says about Erhardt, how he wants revenge. The guy's Italian and if somebody hurts him or his family, look out!

He puts a curse on this Erhardt. He does, he puts a curse on the guy.

Well, I don't know much about curses, but shortly afterwards, the department changes its rules and does away with the rank of acting sergeant. This Erhardt becomes an ordinary patrolman again, losing his sergeant's pay. I don't know if it had anything to do with my father's curse. . . .

4

THE first time I came up against a defense attorney was in a narcotics case. Cops, when they're testifying, get hell from defense lawyers. It's the job of the attorney to be hard on the patrolman giving evidence against his client, but some of them are brutal. Brutal and unfair.

One night tour, at Eighth Avenue and 133rd Street, I see figures moving in a hallway. I step closer and, through a glass door, I see a guy in a gray hat handing over something to two younger fellows. It's got to be junk. I can see the two guys giving money to Gray Hat.

They've put a trash can behind the door, jammed against the handle. I step back and give the door a kick. It flies open and in I go. Gray Hat takes off up the stairs.

"Don't move," I shout. "I'm a police officer. Come down."

He does. I lock up all three of them. They're all carrying junk. I charge Gray Hat with sales felony and the other two with possession. Gray Hat pleads not guilty and gets a defense attorney.

We go to trial in the old felony court in the Criminal Courts building downtown.

I'm on the stand all morning, first being questioned by the assistant district attorney and then by the defense attorney.

65

I look young and inexperienced, and the defense lawyer sets out to discredit me. He implies I'm incompetent and not to be trusted.

The questions come faster and faster as he tries to trip me up.

"How could you see anything in that dark hallway? There was only a dim light, isn't that so, officer? The glass in the door was discolored and grimy. Isn't that right, officer? How long have you been a police officer?"

He put me down so badly that he succeeded in making me feel nervous and unsure of myself. The assistant district attorney later told me I shouldn't let these defense attorneys get to me. But Gray Hat was convicted anyway.

My dad, he came to court when I had to show up there to give evidence. Sometimes he took a day off from work so he could be in court. When I walked in, the first thing I used to do was look round to see if I could spot his bald head among the spectators. He was a tough critic. If I didn't do too well on the stand, he would bring his hand up to hold his nose to show me he thought my testimony stank. If I was nervous and stuttering, there he'd be, slowly shaking his head.

For years, he kept coming to court when I had to be there. One time, there was a case involving two dope pushers . . . I'd bought junk from both of them as an undercover detective. I didn't do a good job of preparing myself for the trial . . . to tell the truth. I guess I was a bit cocky because earlier cases had gone so smoothly. In this instance, I hadn't taken good notes of important things like the time I made the buys and that sort of detail.

The defense attorney was a sharp cookie . . . he knew his business and he tied me up on the stand. He made me fumble for words and he got me so nervous I forgot everything. I was squirming in my seat. By the time he'd finished with me, I was not even sure I made any buys.

The assistant district attorney tried to help me get my wits back by making objections to the questions but the judge kept overruling him.

It looked as if the case was going out the window. I glanced over at my dad, and I could tell by his face he was disgusted with me. Later, my dad told me what happened next. He said the man sitting next to him in the spectators' seats leaned back and said loudly, "That cop's a liar!"

My dad got up in the middle of the courtroom and he grabbed this man's jacket and he started shaking the guy as hard as he could. "You sonofabitch," he shouted. "What you mean he's a liar! He's no liar." And he went on shaking this guy until his teeth rattled.

The whole courtroom, including me, turned to look at all this and the judge stopped the hearing. He ordered the court attendants to put my dad and this guy out of the courtroom.

Out they went and the judge decided to cool everything off by recessing the hearing until 2 P.M. The defense attorney objected to this because he knew he had me on the run and he didn't want me to have a chance to collect myself. But the judge stayed with his decision and the courtroom was cleared.

Wow. Was I pleased. It was just the break I needed.

In the corridor, I saw my dad and, boy, was he pissed off. He looked at me and he said, "You know, Anthonee, you stink! You some big-shot cop!" The other cops, who worked on the case with me, they smiled at each other and I felt like a little boy again.

"Come on," my dad said, "we all go and have lunch. I buy it."

I could never get my dad to admit it, but I'm sure he

created that disturbance to get me off the hook the defense lawyer had into me. When I asked him if he did it on purpose, he just smiled and he wouldn't say anything.

When he got sick and had to go to a hospital, he wanted to know about the court cases I appeared in, and he gave me advice about how to handle myself with the lawyers. My dad, who never went past third grade. He's gone now, and there's no bald head for me to look out for when I walk into court. It's not the same.

Another day, I'm downtown in the criminal court to testify on one of my arrests and I see this guy staring at me from the public seats. I finish my evidence and I'm walking out of court when this guy comes up to me. He identifies himself as a police captain. He wants to know how old I am and how many arrests I have.

I tell him and he wants to know how many of the arrests are for narcotics. "About 75 per cent," I say.

"How would you like to be an undercover agent?" he says. "In the narcotics division."

"Man," I say, "I sure would."

A couple of weeks later, I get a call to go down to the narcotics division. I'm interviewed and everything, but then nothing happens. The usual bull, I think. Finally, I mention it to Captain Forth. I'm real hot to become a detective and this is one way to go. He telephones the narcotics division.

"I have an officer here," he says, "who would be very useful to the division. He has a high arrest record and he's a good all-round man." A couple of days later, I was called down to the narcotics division and interviewed again.

One day in June, 1960, I walk into my stationhouse and see a chalked message on the blackboard, telling me to report to the clerical officer. The clerical guy looks at me and says,

68

"Okay, junkie cop, you've got it. You're being transferred to narcotics."

Wow!

A lot of the guys come and shake my hand because they know how much I want this assignment. I feel great. I run to the telephone, my uniform on its hanger on my back, and I call Helen. I gabble the news and she gives a little shriek, she's so happy for me. I spend so long talking, I'm late going on duty.

My dad is the happiest. He wants us to go out for a drink to celebrate. But Helen's mother has cooked a meal, a feast, so I have to put that off until the next day. Helen's dad, though, he's not all that pleased.

"I think you might have made a mistake," he says seriously. "That's a dirty job. And it's a dangerous job." But I don't care. Now I've got my chance to make detective.

A few days later, I join the narcotics undercover unit. First off, I'm sent out with a seasoned undercover man, Jimmy O'Malley, a black-haired Irishman, always with a smile on his baby-face. His father is a sergeant in the 32nd Precinct where I've come from so, of course, I know about Jimmy O'Malley. He's a sharp guy on the street. He knows his business, and we get on well.

He teaches me a lot. Where to carry a weapon so that it can't be found easily if you're patted down. How to apply for money to make buys. How to work with a back-up team. He introduces me to informers and shows me how to work with them. He explains all the paperwork involved in the job.

But the biggest point he makes to me is that an undercover man must be a shadow. "You've got to be inconspicuous," he says. "Never draw attention to yourself, either by your clothes or by your actions. You've got to become almost

69

invisible . . . an invisible junkie because you're so ordinary-looking, so unnoticeable."

I'm impatient, having to work with another man, but he laughs and says, "Take it easy, Tony, take it easy. You'll get on your own." I want to make my first buy on my own and in a couple of months I do.

An undercover detective has to make at least two buys from a pusher before that pusher can be arrested. This is to show a pattern, that the pusher is in business.

I make some small buys and then I'm teamed up with back-up detectives in the Bronx, Jack Nelson and Charlie Ransom. Nelson later gets the Medal of Honor. Information has come in that teenagers are buying stuff on 163rd Street, at a dry cleaning store. It's a Puerto Rican neighborhood and I don't speak Spanish, but in this town if you've got money you can buy heroin whether you speak Spanish, Italian or Chinese. I'm hot to go.

For a couple of days, we watch the dry cleaning store and see teenagers going in and coming out. They don't have any clothing when they go in and they don't have any clothing when they come out.

"Listen," I say to Nelson, "I'm going to give it a try. Take care of my gun." I give him my revolver. Sometimes an undercover detective carries a gun; sometimes he doesn't. It depends on his feeling about the situation. Sometimes, I used to carry one stuck down in my crotch. My badge I'd have on a neck-chain under my clothing.

This time I have a knife. I also have a four-day growth of beard, a tattered shirt, dirty pants and a zippered jacket. My shoes are old and scuffed.

Nelson and Charlie Ransom can't get too close to the store. They have to park a couple of blocks away, but Nelson has a pair of binoculars.

70

I walk towards the store. Like a junkie. I shuffle and my head's down and my shoulders are sagging. It's easy for me to act like a junkie because I've seen so many. I look mean and I look sick. Outside the store is a group of Puerto Ricans, speaking Spanish. One of them is using broken English a bit, so I go up to him and I ask if he's seen Lynch. This guy Lynch is a pusher. I know he's not around because he was arrested three days earlier. I know because I locked him up.

One of the guys outside the store, a small junkie called Nickie, is looking to buy heroin himself. I ask them if they have money. I suggest pooling what we've got, so we can get more than if we buy separately. I tell them I've only got a couple of dollars and they say, no deal. Now I've got them bullshitted. They're convinced I'm a junkie.

I stand with them and I watch people going into the store to buy stuff. Then I go in. The guy behind the counter is a tall Puerto Rican with cropped hair, name of Johnny.

"Hey, Johnny," I say, "I'm short. I wanna get some stuff but I'm short." He won't trust me for the difference between the cash I say I've got and the cost of the stuff. He suggests I take less, but I say I need more than I can pay for. He's bullshitted, too.

"I'm gonna crack into some cars and see what I can pick up," I say. Junkies who are short will break into cars, grab property and sell it quick to raise money for their habit.

"I'll be back," I tell him. Cutting through buildings to make sure I'm not being followed, I head back to my team. Nelson says he's seen everything through his binoculars.

I go back later and I'm talking again to guys outside the store. We talk about one thing. Junk. And about how The Man is around and how we've got to be careful.

I look through the window of the store and see Johnny playing checkers. He nods to me and I shrug my shoulders

71

to indicate I have no cash. I go in and ask if I can do some work to make money. He says, no. But he lets me play checkers with him. I beat him . . . he's easy.

We go on playing and every so often junkies come in and buy the white glassine envelopes containing stuff from Johnny. He's getting angry because I'm beating him at the checkers and when I try to let him win, he still loses because he's such a glom.

A patrol car comes by and slows in front of the dry cleaning store while the two patrolmen riding it stare at the junkies hanging around. The junkies get the message and drift away.

Johnny says, "Cool it. The Man is out there. Get outta here."

I go outside and one of the cops comes over to me and grabs me by the shoulder. He starts shaking me and he says, "Didn't we tell you to move off?"

"Hey, man," I say, "I live over here." That's all I have to say.

"What did you say?" the cop demands. "What did you call me?"

"Officer," I say.

"You didn't call me that," he says and, whack, he smacks me in the jaw.

He throws another punch and I put up my arm to fend him off. His fist slips off my arm, I give him a push and then I start running. The two cops chase me, but it's easy. I cut down an alley and there's a guy sitting on a fence who says, "Hey, man, go this way!" He knows the cops must be after me and he directs me into a building from which I can get onto the avenue.

I go back to my back-up team. Jack Nelson and Ransom are laughing—they saw the cop punch me.

Next day, I go back with money to see Johnny at the dry cleaner's. He says, "What you want?"

I say I need a lot of stuff. I've got to find out where his connection is.

"All right," he says, and he gives me an address on Stebbins Avenue. "Go up to the first floor, knock and tell the broad I sent you."

That's what I want to know . . . where the stuff is coming from. It's got to be coming from this apartment. I go to the address Johnny gives me on Stebbins Avenue. It has a dirty hallway, with a broken glass door and glass on the floor. When I knock, the door cracks open and there's a small Puerto Rican woman, about twenty-one years old. Pretty.

I say, "Johnny sent me. I need two bundles." A bundle contains fifteen decks of heroin, cost $75. She lets me into the apartment which is lousy with roaches, and stinks. She goes into a bedroom and comes out with a large package tied with a rubber band.

She unwraps the package and takes out two bundles. I give her the cash and leave with the bundles. In the team's car, we initial the bundles and put them in a police property clerk's envelope which we seal. I initial the seal and on the envelope I scribble the buy number, the time I bought it, the apartment address and the name Jane Doe Orange Blouse because I don't know her name but I do know she's wearing an orange blouse. I take it to the police laboratory downtown and get the stuff analyzed.

I go back and make a buy from Johnny, telling him I need more. I give him $50 and he tells me to go to the corner of the block. While I'm standing on the southeast corner of Rogers Place and 163rd Street, a guy comes up and says his name is George.

"You see Johnny?" he asks.

"Yeah," I say.

"Okay," he says, "here's the stuff." He gives me a package.

Me and my team, we then go north to Third Avenue in the 170s, another big junk area. I'd seen some activity earlier in front of a building on Third Avenue and I want to get in on it. I put on a black beret and pull my hair out at the sides. I walk with a hunch. I look like a real drag.

The guy I want, a dealer called Eddie, is there. Now I have to make the contact. I don't go right up to him. A few feet away from him, I stick my finger down my throat and make myself throw up. I'm puking all over the sidewalk and over myself, too. It sounds disgusting . . . Pepsi-Cola, which I'd been drinking in the team's car splashing all over the place. Some hits Eddie.

This guy Eddie, he's mad now and he walks away.

"Fuck you," he says, "get outta here." I walk away a bit and then I stop and I heave up again. After a moment, I clean my lips and, staggering very slightly, I go over to him.

"You straight?" I ask.

"Who are you?" he wants to know.

"My name's Solo." I'd hit on that name because it was easy to remember and I felt it described me. A loner.

"What d'you want?" he asks.

"What you got?"

"Three-dollar bags."

"Man," I say, "I've only got $2.75."

"No good," Eddie says.

"Please, man," I say. "I'm sick, you gotta help me. I'll bring you the other quarter."

He looks at me, at my rotten clothes, at the sick on my shoes and he takes out a glassine envelope. He gives it to me and I give him $2.75. Now I'm happy, happy as a junkie who's got a fix. I've got the sonofabitch. I take off and then I go back with the quarter I owe him. I tell him I'll see him around.

About a week later, I make another buy from him. As well as from Eddie, I make buys from six men and the woman, all connected to the dry cleaning store. I buy a total of 180 decks of stuff. Now we have to make the arrests.

I give descriptions to Jack Nelson and Ransom. They go to the dry cleaning store and bust Johnny and another guy with him. They take the two to the 41st Precinct and come right back on the street. I tell them they missed a guy who's still there, and, zap, they grab him. This is Nickie. They take him back to the stationhouse, too.

While they're away, I'm standing on the corner with other junkies. "Hey," they say, "we'd better split. It's hot. There's a rat around here." Everybody's looking at one another. They seem to be looking at me especially.

"Yeah," I say, "there is. Let's take off."

My team comes back and we make a meet away from the store. Now there's nothing. The streets are clean.

Jack Nelson and Ransom want to go back to process their prisoners. "Don't leave," I say. "Let's stay on the street. They'll come around."

But they've got all that paperwork to do and they leave. They tell me, "Don't hang around. Get off the street—it's dangerous." I stay on the street anyway. I'm walking around and I meet a junkie named Tun-Tun. I try to buy from him, like I have before, but he doesn't want to know.

"Get off the street," he says. "It's hot." I see him go into the apartment on Stebbins Avenue. I slip into a doorway and keep watch on the entrance. Orange Blouse goes in. Others start drifting in.

75

I call the precinct and tell them to get down there quick. Four detectives, including Nelson and Ransom, show up. They want the descriptions, but I say, "No good. Take me into the apartment. Make believe I'm a prisoner. Cuff me and hold me under the arm. When we're close to anybody who sold me junk, I'll squeeze your hand with my arm."

We go to the apartment and the team kicks the door down. There's a dozen people in the apartment and the detectives line them all up. There's a second woman with a two-year-old baby. Every time we pass a dealer, I give Nelson's hand a squeeze with my arm and he makes the collar.

A paddy wagon arrives to take the prisoners. The team can't find any stuff at first but then they open up a camera and find junk in it. They ask Orange Blouse why she's selling narcotics.

"I sell dope because my husband, he's in jail and I want bail money to get him out."

"Why's he in jail?"

"He's in jail because he sell dope."

It's a successful raid. This gang of pushers has been selling to the entire neighborhood, including kids in the nearby school. They've also been selling to other pushers in other areas. In fact, they think I'm a pusher from somewhere else in the South Bronx.

The junk I've bought probably comes from Turkey or Southeast Asia. Along the way, it's been whacked up, or diluted, time after time after time. When it arrives in this country, it's pure heroin. When it reaches the street junkie, it's been whacked up with quinine or sugar at least ten times so that each person in the chain of distribution can take an enormous profit, charging heroin prices for the dilutant.

The big connection who stands at the top of the pyramid

—and there are many top connections at the top of many pyramids—could be a banker, a lawyer, a businessman, who never sees the stuff.

He merely invests, say $100,000, on which the return could be $500,000. This big connection is almost impossible to reach because he's so far removed from any actual dealing. Underlings superintend the smuggling of the heroin, often by the kilo, which amounts to 2.2 pounds.

From them, it goes to other connections—after it's been diluted once. These lower connections might pay $25,000 and up for one kilo. They whack it up again.

Down the chain of distribution it goes to other connections, who might buy an eighth of a kilo, up to half a kilo. Again it's whacked up, but it's still pretty good stuff.

At this level, the connection distributes the junk to maybe five or six lieutenants working for him. Now it's getting close to the street.

These lieutenants run "factories" for further whacking up and bagging of the heroin in glassine envelopes, or decks. If the lieutenant cops from a good junk man, he can whack it up two or three times more. One time I'm taken into a "factory." This is how it operates.

There's a long table in an apartment and the table is covered by smooth glass, which will not absorb the heroin. Working at the table are three or four women, naked so that they can't hide any of the junk in their clothes.

Standing at the door is a guard with a shotgun.

While the lieutenant watches, the first woman at one end of the table opens up the "piece," equal to one ounce, costing $700. She mixes in milk sugar or quinine to dilute it. Quinine is best because it helps give the junkie the rush of euphoria when he shoots up.

She fluffs up the mixture, letting in air so that it appears to be more than it actually is. The next girl has two-inch-square envelopes, which she fills with a couple of grains to make a five-dollar bag.

The third girl places this deck inside another envelope and passes it to another girl, who tapes it closed and wraps a rubber band around it. They're all junkies and they get paid off with heroin, enough for one or two days, depending on their habit. The same with the guard.

A number of these bags are put together to form what they call a "bundle," or a "load."

Now, the street pusher takes over. He'll pick up, maybe, fifteen bags. He sells twelve bags, at $5 each, which nets $60. He must turn in this $60, but he can keep three of the bags for himself.

If he doesn't pay off, forget it. They'll kill him. If the street pusher decides to whack it up further to make more profit, then he can be in bad trouble, too.

This pusher may sell to other pushers, or he may sell directly to the junkie on the street. An operation can be far more complex than this, but it gives the general idea. Also, any figures and amounts are constantly changing because of inflation or the shortages which cause panic in the street.

The profits are enormous all the way down. The raw opium grown in Turkey may be sold by a peasant for $500. When that junk reaches the streets of New York, it sells for more than $500,000.

After the dry cleaning store job, my bosses are pleased with me, but I still want Eddie on Third Avenue. Like all the other dealers, he's off the street because it's hot. But, after a few days, I spot him. I tell my team to stay on Third Avenue and I'll bring him out where they can grab him. He's coming out of a store eating a pretzel and drinking a Coke.

"Hi, Eddie," I say, "what's happening?"

"Nothing, man," he says. "Get the fuck away from me. I'm clean, I have nothing. Don't you know The Man is around? Get off the goddam street."

"Take it easy," I say. "I'm just looking to cop some stuff."

"I don't want to know nothing," he says, real tight. "Get outta here."

He walks off and I start to follow him. He turns around and says, "Hey, fucko, what're you following me for?"

I know I'm drawing a tip by doing this, upsetting him, so I have to come up with a story. "Listen, Eddie," I say. "Maybe you can help me out. I've got about $600 cash on me. I wanna cop."

He stares at me and his eyes get greedy. Sure he'll help me cop. Of course, what he really has in mind is that he'll take that $600 off me. I know the connections are on Third Avenue so we're both happy, because that's where my team is waiting for me.

"Yeah, man," he says. "I know a dude who's got a lot of stuff, good stuff." He thinks I'm a real glom.

When we get to Third Avenue, he puts his left arm around my shoulders. I know this is bad.

"Solo," he's saying as he clasps me, "of all the guys who come around here, you're the only gentleman I meet. You're real trustworthy. You're not like the other motherfuckers who come around trying to take advantage of us guys."

I know what's going to happen. His right hand is in his pocket and I know he's going to pull something out and it isn't going to do me any good. We stand on the corner, looking for a connection, and I can see the car with my team less than half a block away.

I can't escape because his arm's around my shoulder and he's holding me tight. I'm worth $600 to him. We look in through the window of a bar and now I'm sure he's got a knife in his hand, which is still in that pocket.

Trying not to let him see, I signal to my team to come quick. Nelson catches wise. I hear the car start up and, oh, man, it sounds beautiful. As the car starts to roll, out from Eddie's pocket comes the blade. It's coming up to my throat when the car squeals up and the doors fly open and here comes Jack Nelson with his gun drawn. The blade is inches from my throat when Jack puts his gun to Eddie's head and says, "Drop it!" The knife hits the sidewalk.

They cuff Eddie and me together and put us in the car. When they accuse us of being pushers, I say, "Man, I'm no dope pusher. I just came around to see my buddy here." At the 41st Precinct, they separate us and put Eddie in a cell. He thinks I'm in another cell.

He's booked for narcotics, not for attempted murder, because that would blow my cover. Nelson pats me on the back and says, "Okay, Tony, go on home."

Shortly afterwards, I'm promoted to detective and I get my gold badge. Detective Anthony Schiano.

5

WHEN I was undercover, I was shit scared that one day I'd have to shoot up. I'd have to cook up with another junkie and there'd be no way out of taking a fix.

I've never taken dope and I never will, but, man, I've been around enough times when junkies were shooting up. These guys, they start with one bag of stuff but as their tolerance grows, they need more and more. They'll need two, three, four, five, even six bags at a time.

With the junk, they need the cooker, the cap of a bottle, or a spoon with a bent handle. They put the shit in the cap with some water to dissolve it. Into this, they put a little ball of cotton, usually from the tongue of their shoe, to filter out any sediment. They cook up and draw the junk into a hypodermic needle through the ball of cotton. When they're ready to shoot up, they put a rubber tube or their belt around their arm as a tourniquet.

While they're giving themselves the junk, they'll release the tourniquet. That's when they get the hit. To be sure they get a hit, they put the needle into the vein and wait until some blood oozes up into the needle and then they squeeze the shit into themselves.

Some junkies will boot it. They squeeze some junk into the

vein, then suck some back into the hypo before injecting the full dose. It's disgusting.

I've seen them put the needle in their shoulder, in their jugular vein, in the webbing between their fingers, in their feet. Women will shoot up next to their genitals or on their legs so it won't show on their arms.

After a while, the veins will collapse and you see the black marks on their arms. They'll use the same hole they used the day before, or five hours before. They pick off the little scab so they can put the needle in the same puncture. Eventually, they get an ulcer sore and they have to move somewhere else on their body. You can see junkies with arms covered with punctures and sores.

There's something else about junkies . . . they have a smell on them you won't find anywhere else. A junkie, when he's strung out, he never changes his clothes, never takes a shower. He lives in hallways and greasy basements. It's not like a bad breath smell. It's, maybe, a combination of filth and staleness and urine. You have to smell it to know it.

The way they walk is something else, too. There's a hunch to their shoulders. They walk quick. Their faces have this frown all the time. That's because they're always worrying about their next fix. The thing is, even if you've never taken stuff, when you live with them like I did, you come to the point you have the same kind of sick feeling they have. They have this constant fear they won't be able to get a fix. I have this constant fear I'll be shot or stabbed.

Some cops, some teams I've worked with, they even treat me like a junkie. They don't want to get close to me or be seen with me. It's like they forget I'm a member of the department like them. That I've been through the Academy and patrolled the streets in uniform and gone to communion breakfasts and I've got a good home and a wife and kids in the suburbs. You're with the junkies, so to them you're just another guy looking to cop.

But not to Clancy.

As an undercover detective, I look for back-up teams that are sharp and aggressive. I want guys who don't mind working late, guys who don't mind taking chances, guys who want a lot of collars. Some aren't like that. Detective Tom Clancy is . . . he's a pisser.

He has light red hair, very straight and bristly, a ruddy face which has skin so tight it looks like a skull. But the thing that bothers you most is his eyes.

They're a cold blue and when he looks at you, the hairs on the back of your neck come up and you get a queasy feeling in your gut. When he's talking to the good guys, he always has a joke and a smile, but let me tell you, while he's chatting away, he's studying you.

He's feared throughout lower Manhattan and up into the Twenties on the West Side. The junkies, they fear the very name Clancy. If anyone says, "Hey, Clancy's around," the entire junkie population vanishes. It becomes a ghost town. I'll tell you why . . . he's the meanest fuck in town.

When Clancy approaches a pusher and he knows the pusher is dirty, it goes like this. He stands in front of the pusher and he smiles sweetly at him. Clancy's hands are in his coat pocket, one hand fondling his gun.

Clancy says, "D'you know who I am?" Very quiet.

The pusher says, "Yes, sir."

"Who am I?"

"You're Clancy."

That's it. Clancy chastises him severely, let's put it like that. The dealer recovers from the chastisement after a minute.

Clancy says, "Don't you mean Mr. Clancy?"

"Yes, Mr. Clancy." Clancy smiles at him.

"Give it up," Clancy says. Very quiet again.

The pusher comes up with a package in his hand and he gives it to Clancy, who then makes the collar. The pushers and the junkies, they sure know Clancy.

His partner is Detective Matty Chang, one of the first Chinese guys in the department. Matty's a real sharp dresser, a good-looking guy. He approaches pushers when he knows they're dirty and he says, "I Matty Chang. I Detective Chang," before he chastises them. Sometimes, the pusher is so taken aback, he falls over.

"I Detective Chang," says Matty. "You give up stuff." The dealer hands it over and there's another collar.

They hide in stores and peer through the shades with binoculars. They watch junkies approaching the pusher to buy stuff, maybe two or three of them. They zap out and they collar the junkies maybe a couple of blocks from the pusher. When they've got them, they go and pick up the dealer. Whammo, four arrests at one time.

Clancy and Chang, they come out of shadows, out of hallways, out of cars, and the pushers freeze because they know this is it. It's always the same. "D'you know who I am?" When the pushers hear that, they shit a brick.

Clancy comes to me and he says he has good information in lower Manhattan. Would I team up with him and Matty Chang? I'm busy at this time, working with a lot of other teams, so I don't say yes or no. I want to know if he's got an informer, a junkie working off an arrest because he can introduce an undercover detective to the scene and to the pushers. If I've got to go on the street cold, it's much tougher to make buys because the pushers don't know me in their neighborhood. Junkies usually walk in pairs. The saying is that an addict begets an addict.

84

Clancy says he can get me an informer, but he never does. However, he's persistent and finally I say, okay, I'll work with him. We arrange to make a meet on the second floor of the 10th Precinct.

Before I go in, I have to make sure there's no junkies around in the street who might see me going into the stationhouse. Clancy and Chang are on the block, but when they see me coming, they go inside.

I've got a four-day growth of beard, a straggly mustache and long hair. I'm wearing a black beret, like a lot of Puerto Ricans are wearing at this time. I'm in tattered old clothes and beat-up shoes.

At the top of the steps of the stationhouse is a big patrolman in uniform. As I start to go in, he sticks his hand in my chest and says, "Where d'you think you're going, buddy?"

"I wanna see the detectives."

"What about?" he says. "What's your complaint?"

I look over his shoulder and there's Clancy coming. "Okay, officer," he says, "he's with us." Clancy is getting a charge out of me being stopped. I like it, too, because it means the patrolman doesn't see me as a cop but as some guy off the street. If he sees me as some sort of an undesirable, then the junkies will see me the same way.

We go up to the second floor, where the detectives hang out. Clancy's a joker. He and Chang go quickly into the squad room and then slip into a side room. I start to follow them and, immediately, up jump three detectives who don't know me.

"What d'you want, Mac?" they demand.

"I'm with Clancy and Chang."

"What're you talking about? Where's Clancy? He ain't here."

"He just went into that side room," I say.

They give me a hard time and the next thing you know we're shouting at each other. Only then does Clancy appear, a big grin on his red mug, and he says, "Okay, let him in. He's with us."

We sit down in this crummy interview room and I tell Clancy he should have stayed with me. He makes a big joke out of it, and finally I ask him what he's got. This guy's fantastic. He knows the name of every pusher in the area. Around 13th Street, 17th Street and 22nd Street, he says, there's Princess, a black fag; Pinocchio, who's got a long nose with a pimple on the end of it; Pete and Gracie and Sonny, a young Italian kid with bright red hair. But most of all, he says, he wants to get Mato and Mato's woman who specialize in selling to kids in the area. Also, he wants Jimmy and Eugene and Al.

"How the hell are we gonna do it?" I ask. "I'm going in there cold and it's going to take forever. I got other boroughs to cover."

"Do your best," he says. He has a way of persuading you.

"What kind of cover are you gonna give me?"

"The best," Clancy says. "I'll cover you like a blanket."

But I know they'll have to stay at least two blocks away if it's going to work . . . especially with me going in cold. And two blocks is like being two miles away because you can get a knife in the back before they even start moving.

I go to 17th Street, between Tenth and Eleventh Avenues.

The whole block is alive with junkies. I walk west, checking the scene, trying to make contact. I have to work out who's selling and who's buying. There's a guy leaning against the wall. I know straight off he's a junkie, and I know he's sick, waiting for his connection. Our eyes meet and now there's contact.

86

"Hey, man, you wanna cop?" he says. "I'll get it for you. I know where we can get good stuff. We'll go down together. Okay?" What he's saying is that we both pool the money we've got, buy some shit, cook it and shoot up together.

"No, man," I say. "I'm short."

"How much you got?"

"How much you got?" I come back.

"Like, four dollars," he says. The bag he wants to buy is five bucks.

"I've only got $1.75," I say.

"That's too little for me," he says.

"Can't I put my money with you?"

"No, it's not enough. Let me borrow the money from you, man, and I'll pay you later." He's desperate, you can see it. He gives me his name.

I tell him, "Listen, pal, you got four bucks. I'm keeping my dollar. Here, take seventy-five cents. This way, you talk to your connection and you'll only be a quarter short."

He nearly kisses me when I give him the seventy-five cents. He runs off and I continue walking. That's good. I've made my face known to one junkie. Further along, I get the high sign from another guy that he's got junk. He's got two guys with him as guards, to make sure nobody mugs him for his money or his dope.

"You looking for something?" he says.

"Yeah," I say, "but I'm light. I'm looking to crack a short. How much are your bags?"

"Five," he says.

"I'm short," I say. "I've only got two bucks. Let me give you the two and I'll bring you the three later on, after I crack a car."

He's disgusted. "What! Are you kidding me?" he says.

"Get the fuck outta here. You going light on me three bucks? Shit, no."

This is good, too. He's convinced now that I'm a junkie trying to cop like all the rest, even if he hasn't seen me before. He's sure I'm not The Man. As I walk away, I feel their eyes on me and I try the doors of parked cars all the way along the street, pretending to try to crack into them.

That's the way I go all over the area, making contacts, bullshitting junkies and pushers. Some of the junkies are pressured, looking for a fix bad.

"You wanna go down with me, man?" they say. "I got the cooker, the works."

Most junkies don't carry the cooker with them because if it's found on them, that's an automatic collar. They'll try to find someone else who has the works and they say, "Let me use your cooker and I'll give you a taste of my shit."

I walk for miles, all over the area, letting them see me, talking, spreading a few cents and cigarettes. I have a mean look on my face. I don't look good. I look like a junkie and these street animals, they believe I'm just another guy looking for a fix. I'm on the street for more than three hours.

When I get back to Clancy at the precinct, he's out of his bird. "Where the fuck have you been?" he yells. "Why didn't you come back to the car?" He's real pissed off.

"You knew what I was gonna do," I say.

"Yeah, but you didn't say you were going all over," he screams. "You've been away hours." I guess he's a bit worried about me. But I don't want them within sight of me because if the pushers know Clancy's around, their operation goes into the basements and hallways.

I don't want this because I shit if I have to go into a hallway. To tell the truth, my gut tightens if I have to walk

88

into a side street to make my buy. It's too easy to find a knife coming at you and no way out.

The days go by and I become well known among the junkies. I always carry a pack of cigarettes on me, in my shirt pocket so it bulges noticeably. Even though normally I don't smoke, I would stand on the street corner puffing away and they'd always come up to me, the junkies.

"Hey, man," they'd say. "You gotta cigarette?"

If you gave one junkie a cigarette, then they'd all come around. "Hey, man, you got one for me?" and you'd make another contact. At that time, the cigarette packs didn't have the little message that smoking is dangerous to your health.

The more I became known by the junkies, the more the pushers trusted me because they accepted me as a street guy.

This day in October I'm on a street corner with a junkie who's just bummed a cigarette when I see Princess, this black fag who has dyed red hair and a yellow earring in his left ear. Junkies are going up to him and giving him money and getting little envelopes.

"Are you gonna cop from him?" I say to my junkie. "Is his stuff good?"

"Yeah, his stuff's all right," the junkie says. "But I'm short."

"How much you short?" I say.

"Man, I'm short about $2. He's got $6 bags."

"Listen," I say, "I've got $7. I'll give you a buck so you're only a dollar short and we'll buy together."

We go up to Princess, who recognizes the junkie but not me. "Say, Princess," the junkie says, "will you give us two bags for 11 bucks?"

Princess looks at me and says, "Who's the other guy?" He's got sort of a lisp.

"He's all right," the junkie says. "He's my buddy. We been cracking shorts but we're a dollar light."

"When will you give me the other dollar?"

"Soon as we shoot up. We're gonna sell some stuff."

Princess says okay, and we buy two bags. I notice he's looking at me peculiar, taking me in. "Hey," he says, "I wanna talk to you." He's really got some lisp.

He takes me away from the other guy and he says, "I never saw you around here before. Who are you?"

"What d'ya mean?" I say, a bit nervous now. "I got a girl on 17th Street and I'm doing my thing with her."

"Funny," he says. "I never seen you before. Who d'you know around here?"

"I don't know nobody," I say. "I come from uptown around 117th Street and the Bronx. It got too hot in the Bronx and the shit got bad on 117th Street. Then they started beating up on us."

"Well," he says, "I don't live too far. If you wanna come up to my house, you can shoot up there and you're welcome to it."

You know what he meant? The guy dug me.

"Okay," I say, "where d'you live?" The guy gives me his address. Beautiful. After I buy from him again, I'm going to send the team right round to his house to lock him up. It couldn't be better.

I tell him I'm going to shoot up with the junkie and we get away from him. "Ta-ta," he lisps. "Fuck you," I say to myself. But there's still trouble because now my junkie expects me to shoot up with him. "We can cook up together," he says, "and there'll be more for us that way." I'm not shooting up with anybody, but how do I get away from him without drawing a tip?

90

We're walking south on Tenth Avenue and suddenly I see the team in their car about a block and a half away.

I don't expect to see them, but this Tom Clancy's great. He knows the way the junk is going and there he is. I see the binoculars shining through the windshield and I think, wait a minute, now I know how to get out of shooting up with this junkie. I'll deliver him right to Clancy.

As we get near the car, the junkie spots the team and he says, "Oh-oh, there's The Man."

"Take it easy," I say. "Slow down." We saunter by but the junkie is as nervous as hell.

"Hey, fucko," he says, "let's go." I try to calm him, and finally he says, "Yeah, yeah, you're right." We keep walking slow. Clancy's watching us, waiting for a sign from me.

"Let's make believe we're looking in this store window," I say. "We gotta be nonchalant or they'll take us." Again he agrees. As we stare into the window, I gesture behind my back at the junkie, telling Clancy he's got stuff.

I hear car doors open and slam behind Clancy and Chang. I hear their footsteps coming until they're right behind us. In the window I can see the reflection of Clancy and Chang standing there. The junkie knows it, too.

They tap us on our shoulders and we turn round. I almost burst out laughing, looking at Clancy's red face.

"D'you know who I am?"

"Yes, yes," the junkie stutters, "you're Mr. Clancy. Here, I got it, here it is." And he hands over his dope. He goes on, "Listen, this guy's got stuff, too, he's dirty as well. It's in his right-hand pocket!"

The little fuck has turned me in! He informs on me to Clancy.

The team puts us in the car and takes us to the stationhouse, where the junkie goes into a cell and I start the formalities of all the paperwork. Sometimes I think I'd rather sit in a cell.

Over the next days, I buy from Sonny, Pinocchio, Pete, Gracie, Al, Eugene, Jimmy, Bluecoat, Mato's woman, she's the one who carries the stuff either in the crotch of her panties or in her bra because cops are reluctant to search a woman in the street. But, let me tell you, not Tom Clancy . . . he'd search anybody.

Early in November, I approach Mato on 15th Street, outside a five-story building. He's very cautious and mean, so you can't approach him except one at a time.

I don't say a word . . . I just show him one finger, which means I want one bag of stuff. He nods and I hand him $4, after which he sends me into the hallway of the building where Mato's woman is. She pulls down her dirty panties, takes out the envelope and gives it to me. I get away and immediately go to a bar to wash my hands . . . she's no bargain.

Later, I buy from Mato again and altogether I've bought from about a dozen pushers. It's time to make the collar.

It's going to be a long day for me and Clancy and Chang. We make a meet in the 10th Precinct. The detectives on the second floor, they know me now and they treat me good with coffee and so on. A bunch of good guys. I make Clancy promise that when he picks up a pusher, he's got to come straight back on the street from the stationhouse. I have problems with some teams. They make a collar and then they go back to the precinct and do all the processing while I'm still out on the street. It takes them an hour, and all that time I'm out waiting for them, seeing other pushers I want grabbed.

This is the most dangerous time for me because once a

team starts making collars, the dealers know there's a rat around, an undercover detective who's fingering them. The first guy they look for is the new face on the block, and if they decide it's me, well, forget it. . . .

Clancy and Chang agree to do it my way. That settled, I tell them where we'll operate . . . Bickford's, a big restaurant on 23rd Street and Eighth Avenue. This was where the junkies gathered in the mornings to wait for their connections so they could get their morning fix. They're all there, waiting, inside Bickford's and on the sidewalk outside. It's a very busy intersection, with lots of pedestrians and subway stations on each corner. Bickford's is on the southwest corner and I see Clancy and Chang taking a position on the northeast corner where the junkies can't spot them.

They're sitting in Matty Chang's car and they've got binoculars.

I'm very nervous with that old queasy feeling in my gut. But, as well as the fear I've got that excited feeling . . . the excitement of the chase . . . of the capture. I see Pinocchio and make a mental note of what he's wearing so I can pass the information on to Clancy and help him spot the guy. I don't talk to anybody. I just walk slowly away, wait at the intersection for the lights and stroll on towards the team's car.

Approaching the car, I nod for Clancy to follow me and he smiles because he knows I've got a collar for him. I keep going and I hear the car door bang behind me. I duck into a building and Clancy follows me in.

I'm in my ratty clothes but Clancy, he looks good. He's crisp and sharp in a gray pin-stripe suit and spotless white shirt. He smiles at me and says, "What've you got, Tony?" He's real eager, this guy Clancy.

I tell him what Pinocchio is wearing and where he is. He's

93

hot to go. "Now, wait a minute, Tom," I say, "don't do to me what those other guys do. You take him in and then come right back on the street. It's dangerous on the street and, besides, I need you for more collars."

He says okay. I go back to Bickford's, which has two entrances, one on the avenue and another on 23rd Street. Inside, I take a seat near the big plate-glass window. Now the excitement has me by the throat . . . I always get that feeling, even today, when I'm making an arrest. It's like flying, I guess, or jumping out of a plane when I go skydiving.

Clancy has stayed behind in the hallway. From my window seat, I see him come out after a few minutes and go to Matty Chang's car, a late-model Torino with a high-powered engine and a beautiful panel dashboard. This Matty Chang surely knows how to live. My team sits in the car, but they don't drive up yet . . . Clancy's real sharp. I know what he's doing. He's got his binoculars, looking for Pinocchio.

Pinocchio's moving around a lot inside and then, beautiful, he decided to go outside. As soon as he appears, Matty Chang starts his car. The Torino waits for the lights, then swings round, not too fast, in front of Bickford's.

Some of the junkies recognize the car immediately and start to move off, but others don't. The car stops on the crosswalk and out come Clancy and Chang. Now they all know. Inside, guys are standing up at their tables and peering out.

"Hey, Clancy's here," they say.

Clancy walks over to Pinocchio, who starts gesturing with his arms. Oh-oh, I think, Pinocchio's making a mistake. Clancy chastises him very severely. It's so severe that Pinocchio looks quite groggy and they have to help him into their car. They take him off to the stationhouse.

94

The word spreads that they've picked up Pinocchio . . . the guy with the good stuff, he's gone. Now what d'we do? But they're not scared. They know the procedure of arrest as well as anybody . . . that Clancy's got to process his prisoner before he can come back out again. Besides, they've got to get their morning fix, they've got to find another connection now that Pinocchio's gone.

Two other pushers I've bought from, Pete and Gracie, they show up and, soon after, I see Clancy and Chang return to their parking spot across the intersection. I leave and head back to repeat the meet with Clancy in the hallway. He listens as I describe what Pete and Gracie are wearing and he's smiling again because here's two more collars for him.

I go back to Bickford's and, lo and behold, yet another pusher has shown up, a young Italian boy, Sonny, but of course the team doesn't know he's there. The Torino comes back to Bickford's, and this time Clancy and Chang come inside. Everybody's seen them, of course, and Sonny, he moves to the back, near the 23rd Street entrance.

Clancy and Chang go straight over to Gracie, who's sitting down with some other girls. Without saying a word, they grab her hands so she can't ditch any stuff and cuff her. When they turn to Pete, he's got his fly unzipped because that's where he's got his stuff and he wants to get rid of it quick. Too late. Clancy hears the noise of the zipper and he knows that's where Pete keeps his stuff because I've already told him.

Clancy chastises him and reaches in to pull out the stuff from under Pete's genitals. The team takes the pair off to the stationhouse.

After that, the junkies and pushers know there's an undercover cop around. Bickford's cleans out. Sonny goes south on Eighth Avenue and when Clancy comes back, I go after Sonny, followed by the team about a block behind me. I go into hallways and stores, but I can't find him. Then, at 15th Street, I see him near a diner.

"Hiya, Sonny," I say.

"Hey, watch yourself," he says, "Clancy's around."

"Listen, are you straight?"

"I can't do nothing now."

"Sonny, please," I say, "I'm sick." I want him to go to his stash, with me along, so that Clancy will know he's the guy we want. But he won't. He keeps going south, with me following. As we walk along, other guys come out of doorways and ask Sonny for stuff. We're all walking . . . it's like the Pied Piper.

Finally, he agrees to sell to us and turns around to go north on Eighth Avenue, back towards Clancy. But now I've got to get rid of all these other guys who want to cop. They're going to be in the way.

"Sonny," I say, "what're you doing? We've got six guys following us . . . we're going to get picked up. Tell them to wait and we'll bring back the stuff. You don't have to take their money. Just take orders and then bring back the right amount of stuff."

He agrees and tells the other guys to wait in a hallway. He takes their orders, just like some guy going for take-out items at a luncheonette. We go on then, just the two of us. In the middle of the block, he goes into a hallway, telling me to wait outside on the sidewalk.

When he comes out, he says, "Okay, what d'you want?"

"Just a bag," I say, and he gives me one. I give him $6. He says he's got to get more stuff somewhere else, so we go further north. At 20th Street, we're waiting for the light when the team's Torino pulls up right in front of us and out come Clancy and Chang.

"Oh, my God!" Sonny says. We're both stuck in the car and taken to the stationhouse. There, I'm put in a cell with Sonny and the other pushers who've been grabbed. They're all mad as hell.

"There's a rat around," one of them says. "Somebody turned us in . . . it has to be a rat. Who is it? If we get him, we'll cut him good." I suffer a bit of diarrhea.

"Yeah," I say. "There's gotta be a rat. Hey, I saw Eugene running in and out of Bickford's, the guy with the bad front teeth."

One of the pushers, he agrees. "He's right," he says. "I saw that Eugene going in and out. It's him." They all think it's Eugene.

"That rat bastard!" they start saying. "He did that to us. We're gonna kill that bastard."

I know what Eugene's really been doing. He's been running in and out because he waits for victims at the subway entrance, women whose pocketbooks he snatches. He'll snatch two or three pocketbooks in a morning.

Even so, I'm still not feeling good because one or two of the pushers are giving me the evil eye. I'm beginning to sweat when Clancy comes along and says he wants to question me and he takes me out of the cell. I've been working for twelve hours straight, walking about six miles, and I'm bushed, so I go home while the team processes the pushers.

On my way home, I think about Sonny, the young Italian kid. He's twenty-six, a little bit of a thing. He's like a little boy . . . he talks compassionate, like a priest could have. He's not hard, like the others. He's just a kid who got hung up on stuff and turned pusher to support his habit. I wonder if I can do something for him and later I find I can.

Sonny says he wants to work off his case by becoming an informer, helping me on the street. He doesn't want to go to jail. He teams up with me and we make buys together.

While we're on the street, he tells me all about his life and how he became hooked. I like the guy.

I go and see the priest at the church he belongs to and he comes with me to court. We take the case up with an assistant DA and finally Sonny gets off with a very light sentence.

But you know what he does . . . he takes off on me, the fuck. I don't see him for a year and when I do see him again, he's downtown and he's dead. He dies of an overdose of heroin. It turns out he's going to die anyway because he has a lump on the side of his neck . . . cancer.

Princess, he also becomes an informer. After I make two buys from him, we try to pick him up but Clancy can't find him, even though we've got his home address. Finally, I say, "Screw it," and I go round there on my own. He's in.

He digs me, the fag, and lets me in, thinking I've come for whatever's on his mind, but that isn't what's on my mind. I flash my badge and take him in because me and the team are tired of playing games. Princess wants to work off his case and, since he's not a hard guy and seems honest, I team up with him.

By now, I've made buys from over 200 pushers who've then been arrested by Clancy and Chang. The trouble is they come back on the street too fast. I even make buys again from guys who I've had arrested and come right back out to make some fast bread for their expenses in court. I'm well-known in the neighborhood now. All the pushers and junkies know Tony Solo.

This cold night, I'm on the corner of 23rd Street with a bunch of junkies and we're talking about the usual subject, where to get the best stuff. Across the street I see a guy called Mike the Greek. He's having some sort of argument with a woman junkie, pushing her and slapping her.

I see her hand come up at the Greek's face real fast, and there's an explosion of blood. The same hand comes up again and there's more blood. I know what it is—she's got a little razor in her fist and she's slashed him bad. He screams and falls down while she takes off.

The cops show up and take him to the hospital. When he comes out on the street again, his face is heavily bandaged, covering more than forty stitches. But he's a pusher and even while he's recovering from his wounds, he's selling.

At this time, there's a new group of pushers and junkies in Bickford's—guys who don't know me well and therefore don't trust me.

I have to start convincing them I'm an all-right guy and this one time, I'm sitting with them eating some rice pudding and drinking coffee. At my table is Mike the Greek and a broad when in comes a tall young man, stoned to the eyebrows. Other junkies are sitting around us at other tables.

This young guy is making a lot of noise, throwing the salt and pepper containers on the floor, knocking over the sugar and cursing. Mike the Greek turns to him and says, "Hey, man, cool yourself. You trying to draw a tip on us? Keep quiet."

This dude, he's stoned on goofballs, and he says, "What you say? I'll break your ass." Then he picks up a sugar bowl and brings it down at Mike the Greek, who can't see well because of the bandages. I push the Greek out of the way of the bowl which misses him, ending up on the floor.

Here's trouble. I pick up the napkin holder and I smash it right in the face of the young guy, knocking him over his table. Because he's stoned, he topples over to the floor. Some employees come over and they toss him out of the restaurant. Mike the Greek thanks me.

"You see what happens when you use goofballs," he says. "See how it fucks your mind up. Man, stay away from them. I never touch them . . . I only shoot up stuff."

Here's this guy hooked on heroin and he's telling everybody to stay away from goofballs. Marijuana's bad too, he says.

While he's giving us his views, I hear something and I look around and here comes the goof guy again. Now his coat's open and in his belt I can see he's got a long bayonet. "Oh, shit," I say.

The other guys jump up and scatter. Mr. Goofball is coming right at me, taking out his bayonet. I give him a short snap-kick to his belly. I keep kicking him, kicking the fucker back towards the door.

Then I pick up a chair and I smack it against his body. He gives a big grunt and goes down. After that, I've got to get out of there. I run. I run out, and down the avenue.

Clancy and Chang are outside and they see me, and Clancy follows me, wondering what the hell's going on. I go into a hallway and he comes in after me. I'm shaking as I tell him what happened.

"Tom," I say, "I can't go back in that area. This guy's going to come back looking for me. I don't think I hurt him real bad, even with the chair."

Clancy cooks up a plan. The team and me, we head back to Bickford's, them in the car, me on foot. As they draw up outside, I take up a position across the street from the restau-

100

rant. Clancy goes in and tells the manager there's been a telephone call to the 10th Precinct about Mr. Goofball. He collars the guy and hauls him off to the stationhouse, which leaves me okay to go back to Bickford's.

Outside are all the junkies and they give me a big hello.

"Hey, man," Mike the Greek says, "they just busted the guy with the bayonet."

I'm tough as hell. "He's lucky," I snarl. "He's lucky I didn't bust him." Of course, they don't get my double meaning. But now I'm in with this bunch.

"What d'you want?" the Greek says. "You sick?"

"I'm edgy," I tell him. I give him $6 for a bag and so do some of the others. He goes off and when he comes back, he's got the stuff for us.

"You wanna come to my place and do it?" he asks me.

I tell him, thanks, but I've got someplace else to go. After the incident with the goofball guy, I can make a lot more buys, some of them from a little woman called Jackie.

Just about every undercover detective on the street has made buys from her and had her busted, this little old gray-haired woman. She's still out there selling even today.

After all these buys I've made, comes time to make the collars with Clancy and Chang. We pick up two, three, four, eight pushers. It's a big haul and, of course, the junkies smell a rat—me. They work it out, who's the guy who's new and who's bought from all the pushers who've been grabbed. Tony Solo.

I walk the streets but the few pushers still around, they treat me real cold. This night I'm working with Princess and we're sitting at the counter in Bickford's where there's only three or four other customers. We're at the far end of the counter, which is a bad thing. I should've sat near the door.

Anyway, Princess is drinking tea and I've got chocolate with a nice marshmallow floating on top. I'm wearing a tattered old blue topcoat with a safety pin holding the collar closed.

All of a sudden, Princess nudges my knee and I look up and who do I see walk in but Mike the Greek. He's been arrested by Clancy but he's already out on bail. He's got four or five other guys with him. I look at the other entrance and two women junkies are coming in.

"I don't like it," Princess says. "Something's up. We'd better get outta here."

"We can't," I say, "not with them just coming in." We sit there. One of the broads goes out and comes back with three or four more junkies. I don't think I've been so scared in my life.

Mike the Greek goes over to the night manager, who's cleaning one of the cake shelves and says something. The manager shakes his head. The Greek makes a gesture at the guy's face. Still the manager shakes his head. Mike the Greek grabs the guy's lapels and almost lifts him off his feet. This time, the manager agrees to whatever the Greek wants and the next thing you know he takes out a set of keys and gives them to Mike the Greek, who goes over to the doors and locks them. Both entrances.

Princess digs his nails into my knee. "Oh, my God," he says, "something awful's gonna happen to us." His lisp's still there. Just then, Mike the Greek and the rest of the crew start coming towards us.

"Hey, there, Solo," Mike the Greek says, "what's happening?"

"Hiya, Mike, when d'you get out?"

"I just got out this morning, man."

"That's good."

"Yeah," he says. "Hey, you wanna do something?"

"No," I say, "I already done it. I'm straight."

"What d'you mean, you're straight? I'm not gonna take no money from you. I'm gonna give you a free fix, man. How about coming over with us? We got the stuff, everything."

"I don't want to," I say. "I told you . . . what's the matter with you?"

"I'll tell you what's the matter," he says. "You're a fucking rat, man. That's right, you're a rat. You and that other faggot fuck." I can hear Princess shaking in his boots, his bones rattling, and I'm not doing much better.

I get up and I say, "What d'you mean, man?"

"He's saying you're a rat motherfucker," one of the other junkies chips in.

"Oh, yeah," I say. "Well, I'll tell you something . . ." And while I'm still talking, I turn and grab one of the metal chairs and I fling it right through the fucking plate-glass window of Bickford's restaurant. There's a godalmighty crash and all the glass comes shattering down.

While they're still staring, I move. I jump over tables and chairs and I dive right through the window, landing on my hands and knees. Then I'm up and, man, I'm running. I look back and here comes Princess. We run east on 23rd Street and Princess catches up with me and then he passes me, he's going so fast . . . he's like a racehorse.

"See what you did, you sonofabitch," he gasps as he flies past. "See what you did." We run so fast we lose Mike the Greek and his gang.

"Take it easy, Princess," I say. "They've stopped following us." We slow down and catch our breath. Are we shook up. We're so shook up we have to go in a bar and we each have a double shot of Southern Comfort.

Princess says, "They were ready to kill us. They all had blades, man. One of 'em had a lead pipe and he swung at me as I went through the window after you. He missed me by inches."

Later, I see Princess's photograph among mug shots. He's been arrested for narcotics. Then, years later, I'm on the street and I hear somebody call out, "Hey, you sonofabitch." It's Princess. He comes up and throws his arms around me and kisses me in front of some of my brother officers. By this time, I'm out of undercover work.

We go for a coffee and he tells me what has happened to him. He got into trouble, but then he cleaned himself up and got a job. Now he wants to put his experience to work in trying to help junkies. I do what I can to help him become a social worker.

But that time in Bickford's . . . I tell you, even now, the palms of my hands sweat as I think about it. There's something else. At night, sometimes two or three times a night, Helen has to wake me because of my nightmares.

I keep getting this same dream—a guy, a little guy, coming for me with a knife. It's always the same. It's never happened the way I see it in my dream, but I know it will one day.

6

AFTER Bickford's, the area becomes too hot for me and I move north to the 24th Precinct around Amsterdam Avenue, Columbus Avenue, Broadway and Central Park West. It's a mean area. A prostitute's haven, with a mugger on every corner. Heroin all over.

Here I work on my own, with a new team and no informers. I soon come across a building on West 99th Street that strikes me as a real house of horrors. It's a rooming house with about four hundred rooms and a junkie in every room. Half of them are pushers, the rest addicts. It's like a city within a city, Junkville.

When I start going in there to make buys, I go unarmed. Every time I go in, I'm shitting green. The first time I go in there, I'm heading to make a buy on the fourth floor. I use the rickety stinking old elevator, which is a big mistake.

It stops on the second floor and oh, my God, three guys get in. Without a pause, like it's nothing, one of them throws his arm around my throat and starts squeezing my windpipe.

"Give it up," he says. "Where is it?"

I gasp out, "Wait, man. Take it easy. It's in my right-hand pocket." He doesn't even bother to reach in. He just rips down the pocket and the money falls out.

"Where's the rest?" he says, still squeezing.

"In my inside pocket," I say. They take it all and as the elevator stops at the third floor, they run out. It's that quick. The doors close and the elevator takes me up to the fourth floor where I'm supposed to make my buy. I'm clutching my throat, gasping for breath.

I stagger out and there are a bunch of pushers and junkies dealing. Immediately, one of them comes to me and he wraps his arm around my throat.

"Where is it?" he says. "Give it up or I'll kill you."

"Man, you're too late," I say. "Look at me." He sees my pockets all ripped open and he apologizes. "Maybe next time, huh?" he says.

I get out of that building, my house of horrors, and I make for my team. "Shit on me," I'm saying to myself. "I've got to do something or I might as well quit this job."

Next time I go back I've got a knife, but don't think I'm not still sweating. This isn't visiting the Plaza Hotel.

This time, I'm lucky and nobody mugs me while I'm making my buys. In a number of visits, I buy from something like two dozen pushers on every floor of the building.

My fear's as bad each time I go in, and I can't take much more so I tell the team it's time to make the collars. They begin to pick up the pushers, described by me, as they come out of the building, or they go to rooms where the pushers are and knock down the doors to get them.

The pushers soon know The Man's around and they begin to quit the building before we've picked up all my pushers. I want a guy called Earl, six feet four and 190 pounds, an enormous sonofabitch, with a long thick scar right across his face. The team goes in to pick him up but they go to the wrong apartment and they can't find him.

I'm pissed off. "Come on, you guys," I say, "I'll show you where it is."

I go in ahead of them and point at the right door. They haul off and kick the door in and there's Earl. They drag him off, shouting, to the stationhouse. When they've gone, I decide to take a look around Earl's room to see if I can find out where his girlfriend Fanny is. She's a pusher, too. Maybe, I think, there'll be some letters with an address.

Under the bed, there's a shoe box and in it are some letters, but what interests me more is that he's got a .22 in there. Attached to it is a long tube, a silencer.

I take it with me and go out to wait for the team to come back. While I'm waiting, I go to a basement and test the silencer. It works beautifully. I'm sorry I'm going to have to turn it in. When the team's in position outside the house of horrors again, I go back in to look for Fanny and the other pushers I still want.

By now I know better than to use the elevator. I go up the narrow side stairs, with the gun inside my pants at my crotch. On the landing of the third floor I see two guys and I know they're not going to let me by.

I turn to go back down, but one of them is on me immediately. He grabs my collar from behind and the next minute he has a knife against my throat. "Don't move, motherfucker," he says. "You got it."

"You got me, man," I say. "It's in my left pocket. Take it all."

He reaches into my pocket and takes out a roll of bills, something like $60. "That's all I got," I say.

He turns me around and he smacks me across the jaw. Goddamit, it's the same guy who took me off that first day in the elevator. The first time he took $30 and now he's taking another $60. I'm like a welfare office to him. I know I can't finish off my operation in this building if he's going to take me every time he spots me. And I want the rest of those pushers. I can't take this.

"Get the fuck outta here," he says, pushing me.

He's counting the money and I'm going down the stairs, but as I go I reach into my pants and I take out the .22 with the silencer. I've got to show him the gun so he won't mug me any more. I turn around on the stairs and I look up at him.

"Hey, scumbag," I call. "You. Scumbag."

He turns to me, sees my gun and immediately goes for his knife. I can see the gleam of the blade as he comes for me. He's above me, five feet away, when my gun goes "phut," and then again, "phut," real easy and quiet. I hit him in both legs. He gives a little scream and he falls down like a sack of lead potatoes. He's lying there, clutching his knees. The other guy, behind him, has a knife out, too. He doesn't know what happened to his pal because there's no noise from my gun. He stares down at the groaning guy on the floor, looks at me and then draws back his knife arm and I know he's going to throw the blade at me.

I bring up the .22 again and it's got to be quick. "Phut!" I hit him in the hip. He groans. The knife clatters to the floor and he goes down hard. I take the $60 from the first guy and I slowly go down the stairs. Now I can return to the building for the rest of my pushers and nobody's going to bother me. Quiet, no fuss.

Understand me. I'm no killer or sadist. If I don't slow these two guys up, I can't go back to do my job. I don't kill them . . . I don't think I've ever killed anybody.

I follow the rules but there's also a law of nature and

sometimes you have to fight fire with fire. You fight muggers like these bastards the way they fight . . . no holds barred. You hit below the belt, and not with boxing gloves. You sometimes have to kick and punch and bite and cut. If I'm alone in that jungle and that's the only way I can protect myself, that's the way I'm going to do it. If that means bending the rules, okay, pal, I'm going to bend them. Somebody's got to do this kind of work. These pushers can't be allowed to operate unchecked. I do the work the best way I can and this is one of the ways.

I hear later that the two muggers don't go to the hospital. They're taken in by friends.

The scuttlebutt is that they're scared to go to a hospital because the gunshot wounds would draw attention and they know the cops want them, either for narcotics or mugging, I don't know which. Maybe both.

I go back to the building later. Now the word's around that somebody took care of the two muggers and the junkies are pleased because they've all been taken off by these bastards.

I pick up Fanny and the other pushers I've bought from. Each time I go in, I'm sweating. The entire block is a junkie heaven. They have lookout men on every corner, so the team's car can't come close. Even so, I keep going back, going back, until I notice something. The junkies are off the street . . . they've moved their dealing inside the hallways and basements and rooms.

I climb up through the building looking for my pushers, but I get to the top and there's no sign of them. On the top floor, I head for the door leading to the roof so I can come down through the building next door. I have to step over half a dozen bodies.

They're guys who've just had their fixes and gone into stupors. Some have hypos, filled with blood, sticking out of their arms. The high is so strong that it's knocked them all out.

I walk over them, through the door to the roof, then over to the roof door of the next building. I open the door here and, oh, my God, there's about four guys shooting up.

"Who the fuck are you?" one of them says and they grab me and start searching me. I've got the .22 with the silencer in the groin of my pants but they don't look there. It's weird. There's something about searching a man down there. Even cops don't normally search there.

One of them has a nailfile which he holds to my throat, while another goes through my pockets and takes $15. The nailfile is penetrating my skin and I can feel blood oozing. When they've got my money, they let me go. Down on the fifth floor landing, I see a guy, Tee, a pusher who's sold to me twice. He deals to the entire building. When anybody's in need of a fix, they say, "Let's go see Tee. He's up on the top floor."

I'm wondering where his girl friend Minnie Waters is, because she deals too and I've bought twice from her.

Down the stairs I go and out to meet up with my team. I tell them about getting mugged. They don't give a damn. I'll tell you why. When you look like a junkie and you spend your time with junkies, buying stuff and mixing in with all the filth and shit, some cops I work with treat me like a junkie. I don't say all the teams are like that . . . it's just one or two. They have no respect for me.

This team don't even ask if I'm hurt. All they're interested in is making a collar of the pusher Tee on the top floor. I tell them where he is and I say, "Look, when you get him back to the stationhouse, come right back out and take up this position again because I'm going to look for the girl." They go in, take Tee and drive off to the precinct with him. While they're away, I go back into the building to look for more pushers.

I'm standing in the foyer bullshitting with some junkies when a pusher I want comes in. Here's another collar for the team. I slip away and call them at the stationhouse, telling them to get right over.

"Wait a minute," one of the team says. "We're processing our prisoner."

"You come on out," I demand. "You come on out right now because I got another dope pusher for you."

They give me a hard time but I win and they come out on the street again. But when I go in the building again, this pusher has taken off. I go looking for him. He lives on the third floor, so I go up, hunting him.

Goddammit! On the third floor are two of the guys who mugged me earlier and took the $15. They grab me again. They grab me so hard, my left shoulder's sprained.

"What you got?" this guy says. "You gonna cop?"

"Man," I say, "you took all my money. You got it all. I'm trying to get a free fix."

"He's lying," one of them says, real nasty. "Let's cut him." Oh, God, I get scared. Now I get very scared.

"Please, please don't cut me," I say. "I'm gonna crack some shorts [break into cars] and when I come back, I'll take care of you." They argue a bit and then they decide to let me go.

"Okay," one says, "but when you come back, you better give us a taste."

I go back to the team. "Listen," I say, "there's two muggers up on the third floor and I can't get by them to look for my pusher. You gotta get them outta there." They agree.

But when they come back after about twenty minutes, they don't have the muggers . . . they can't find them, they say. "Oh, shit," I say, "now I've got to go back in and they're still around." Once again I'm sweating bad as I go in and up the stairs. The guy I want is nowhere around, not on the third, fourth or fifth floors.

As I'm coming down, a door suddenly opens and these two scumbag muggers come out. They grab me again. I can't take any more of this.

"You got stuff on you?" one of them says. "You got money?"

"I got $3 . . . you're welcome to it." I'm feeling sick.

"Where is it?"

"It's in my shoe," I say. "You took all the rest from my pockets." Actually, I've got about $20 in my shoe, but I slip out $3 and give it to them. I'm thinking that these muggers have to be taken care of or I'll never get the pusher I want.

When I'm going down the stairs, I reach into my pants and I pull out the .22 with the silencer. I want to be very quiet about it, no waves, no nothing. I don't want nobody to call the cops, nothing. I've got to scare them right out of that building.

I sneak back up the stairs and I peer around the corner into the hallways. The two muggers are near the elevator, waiting for anybody who steps out. I know their system. Any junkie who comes off the elevator, they'll say, "D'you wanna cop? We can get good stuff for you." Then they'll have him.

One guy is leaning against the steam. They can't see me because I'm in the dark of the stairwell. It's like a rerun of the earlier thing. Suddenly, the one near the radiator sees me

112

peeking round the corner. The next minute, he's got a gun in his hand. As he brings it up, I can see it's a cheapie Saturday night special. It's like the gunfight at the O.K. Corral. I fire first. "Phut." The bullet hits him in the leg. He moans, grabs his thigh and falls. The other guy says, "What the fuck . . ." and jumps for the gun which is still in the hand of the first guy.

"Phut." I get him in the upper part of his shoulder. He half spins and he falls, too, rolling around on the floor. I take off down the stairs to get the team, but halfway down I stop. I decide to go back up for their gun. It's less than three minutes later that I get back. The two guys have gone and so has the gun they had. I know neither of them is hurt bad. . . . They must have made it down the corridor to their room. This is my chance.

I run down the hallway and bang on the door. The pusher I want, LeRoy, cracks the door. "Are you looking to cop?" he wants to know. "Yeah," I say. "But I'm short $2. Will you trust me?"

I know he won't and he doesn't. "I can't," he says. "I'm on consignment. I can't get more if I don't show money." What's tickling me is that I just shot two guys in his hallway and not LeRoy, not anybody hears a thing.

"I'll come back," I say. "Are you gonna be here?"

"Yeah," LeRoy says. "I'll be here all evening."

"I'll crack some shorts," I say. "When I've sold whatever I get, I'll be back. Within the hour."

Then I go down the hallway, down the stairs and back outside. There's no hassle, nobody knows a couple of guys have been shot. Beautiful. That's what I think at first. Two minutes later, I change my mind.

Suddenly, a tough-looking young patrolman appears in

front of the building. He sees me and half a dozen junkies hanging around the entrance. The next minute, we're up against the wall and he's searching us.

Jesus, I think, he's going to find the gun, and the whole thing will be screwed up. Luckily, he's started the search at the other end. I sneak a look at him, then I reach into my pants for the piece. There's a garbage disposal truck a few feet away with its scoop and jaws open. With a flick of my wrist, I toss the piece into the scoop, breaking into a fit of coughing to cover the clang of the gun landing.

The cop looks along at me when I'm coughing, but he doesn't see a thing. He's got to be new on the job, thank God. He frisked me, finds nothing and tells me to vamoose with the rest.

As soon as I can get to a phone, I call one of my bosses, Sergeant Bob Vaughan, and tell him about the shootings with the silenced gun. I tell him where I dumped it. He says, okay, okay, leave it to him . . . he'll handle it all. He doesn't want me coming in from the street for all the formalities because I'm still needed there and it would blow my cover.

The team takes LeRoy and gradually we take all the rest of the pushers I've bought from. Now nobody's bothering me. I see Vaughan and he tells me the garbage truck was no longer there when he sent round. Also, there's been no report or complaint of any shootings. There's no weapon and there's no complainants. It's a non-event. This Sergeant Vaughan says he doesn't think I'll hear any more about it, but he cautions me to lay off guns with silencers.

Don't think that the collar is the end of the case for me. It's just the start. I have to go to the stationhouse and look at my pushers through a one-way window to identify them and confirm the team has arrested the right guys.

The paperwork starts . . . tons of paperwork. It's the one thing that bugs a detective, all that futzing around with bits of paper. It takes forever.

After the narcotic has been analyzed at the police lab, I have to pick it up and take it with all the paperwork to the indictment bureau downtown. In this room, there's a very long desk and behind that sit three or four district attorneys.

Don't think you just go up and talk to them, like that. You have to fill in another form, a drug form. Then you have to fight the other cops to get a turn with one of the assistant DA's. There's always a line of cops, a mob of them, all waiting. I'd take in coffee and cigars for the DA's to make sure I got quick attention. The other cops, they curse me up and down, but I have to do it because I got so many prisoners to handle.

I tell you, it's like a sale in a department store with everyone grabbing and pushing each other.

When I've told the assistant DA about my case and given him the evidence, he presents it to the grand jury and I testify before them. In every one of my cases, I've come up with a felony indictment from the grand jury.

In the meantime, the arresting officers have taken the prisoner through the arraignment stage. Now this means that when the indictment comes from the grand jury, the pusher still doesn't know who put the finger on him—namely, me.

The indictment accuses him of selling to an undercover narcotics detective on such and such a day at such and such a place. How d'you plead? He tries to think very quickly who the undercover man is, but he doesn't know because he sells to so many guys and we never arrest him immediately after he's made the two sells.

Normally his lawyer, usually legal aid, will work up a deal where he cops a plea (pleads guilty) to possession with intent to sell, which is lesser than a charge of actually selling. You can get 15 years for selling, but only a year or 18 months for possession.

But if he doesn't plead guilty, the case has to go to trial and that's it. Because then I have to appear in court to testify and the pusher knows who the undercover detective is. Tony Solo. After that, he doesn't like Tony Solo one little bit. There's other ways a pusher can fasten on the undercover man who put him away.

Around Amsterdam Avenue, there was a pusher called Bobby Bombita, a mean fuck who always wore a fedora. He sells twice to an undercover detective called Jimmy Ryan, a guy I broke in on the street. Ryan looks like a junior high school student with rosy cheeks and blond hair, a bit pudgy and always with a smile. I tell Ryan he should concentrate on the Village because he doesn't look right for Harlem or the real tough areas.

He's not like me, the way I look. When I'm dressed up in my junkie clothes and my growth of beard, I look real bad and mean and I can get by in most places.

But Ryan's a gutsy sonofabitch and he goes into dangerous neighborhoods like Amsterdam Avenue and Harlem and lower Manhattan and the Bowery to make his buys. On Amsterdam Avenue he makes buys from Bobby Bombita, and Bombita is arrested.

This guy Bombita, his name is Spanish for amphetamine. Some junkies use this amphetamine to mix with heroin and shoot up. This concoction is something. First you get the rush of the amphetamine and then you get the depression of the junk and it blows your brains out.

116

After getting bail, Bombita comes back on the street to start selling again, trying to raise money for his defense.

That's when I see him. I'm working now with a cover team consisting of Detectives Dick Small and Sammy Burger, two top men on the level of Clancy and Chang. They're very aggressive and don't mind working long hours on the street. They're a good cover team.

Bobby Bombita goes into a hallway and I see guys going in and out making buys from him, one at a time. I approach the hallway and see Bobby Bombita with his pants down.

He has a fetish, this guy. He likes to wear women's panties. There he is, with a brown package inside the panties and from this package he's selling white glassine envelopes. He knows me as a face around the neighborhood and I buy two bags of stuff from him for $8.

Bobby Bombita has another thing he's known for. He always carries scissors in his belt at the back. They're not there for cutting his nails.

Sometime later, I see him again on Amsterdam Avenue. "Hey," he says, "what you want? I got one left." While I'm buying from him, he says he's going to skip town because of the case Jimmy Ryan has against him.

When I go back to Small and Burger, I tell them we'd better pick up this Bobby or he'll take off on us, leave the city. The team picks him up and now he's indicted not only by Jimmy Ryan but by me as well. He gets put away.

But about eight months later, I'm walking on Amsterdam Avenue and, shit on me, there's Bobby Bombita out on the street once more. After selling to two cops, here he is on the outside that quickly, and goddamit he's selling again.

I'm wary because I'm not sure if he connected his last

arrest with selling to me a few minutes before the team took him.

But he looks at me and nods and there's no sign he's suspicious, so I buy from him, same price as before. He tells me he's going to leave town because there's a rat in the street. He says he knows who it is. I'm sweating.

"Who is it?" I say.

"Never mind," he says. "When the time is right, I'll get him myself. I'll kill him."

I go back to the team and they're surprised, too, that Bobby Bombita is out. A few days later, I see him again on the street. He's with a bunch of guys. I don't like the way he's looking at me.

"Hey, man," he says, "tell me something. Let's see the marks on your arms. If you want stuff, lemme see your marks." There's only one way out. I act insulted.

"Who said I want your stuff?" I say. "Did I ever say your stuff was good? Let me tell you, it's garbage. But I never said it was garbage. I never asked to see the marks on your arms. I never asked to try your junk first and then pay you. Who needs you anyway? I'm not buying your shit any more."

This slows him up. He hesitates, then he says, "Don't take it so bad . . . I gotta make sure of myself. I'm not selling no more. I know there's an undercover cop out on the street."

I leave them, and don't think I'm not shitting in my pants as I go back to my team. Small and Burger agree with me . . . we've got to arrest this sonofabitch even though I haven't been able to make the two buys . . . only one.

They drive off to look for him, but the team can't find this Bobby Bombita. I'm looking for him too and soon I spot him. The team comes by and I indicate with my eyes that he's over there.

The team's car pulls up with a scream of brakes and opening doors just behind Bombita and his pals. Out come Small and Burger. Bobby Bombita sees them and starts to run, with them after him. It looks as though he might get away, but Small and Burger are something of athletes . . . they play ball and they're in shape. They catch him, cuff him and take him to the precinct to process him.

Now, he won't plead guilty and the case goes to trial, with me having to testify against him.

He's convicted and sent to jail. Okay, I think, that bastard's out of the way.

Then, about two years later, I'm back working Amsterdam Avenue in the 80's. I go into a building on 80th Street, and come across a big guy called Bubba who's selling pot. While I'm buying from him, three guys come in behind me. One of them I recognize. It's Bobby Bombita.

He doesn't see me at first, but I realize I can't get out without going right past him. I'm shitting a couple of bricks. There's about seven other guys there and I'm on my own, no informer, no Jimmy Ryan, nothing.

Bubba hands out our packages of pot and asks Bombita what he wants. At that, Bombita looks over and sees me.

"Hey," he shouts, "that motherfucker's a cop. You just sold to a cop. I was put on trial by him. I did two years for him . . . I'm still on parole." They all look at me and at first they don't believe him. I'm in my usual ratty clothing and they think of a cop as a big guy in a blue uniform swinging a nightstick. Even in my good clothes, I don't look much like a cop, not the usual image of maybe a red-faced Irishman.

Even so, some of them pull out blades. I've got to do something and I've got to do it quick. They have the doorway blocked.

"That's right," I say, tough-like. "I'm a cop." And I stick a hand in my coat pocket and point a finger at them through the cloth of the pocket.

"All right, everybody get against the wall," I say, trying to snarl. "Keep your stuff in your hands. Drop the blades. You're all under arrest. Lean forward with your hands against the wall."

They turn to face the wall, but those with knives are still holding them. It can go either way. Bombita looks over his shoulder at me and he says, "Someday, man, I'm gonna get you. I'll get you, you rat bastard." I'm edging past them towards the door.

"You can try right now," I tell him, "but you're gonna have to catch me." As I say that, I'm through the door, running. Now my hand has to come out of my pocket and they know I don't have a gun. I must've run as fast as Princess did that night at Bickford's, because I lose them and soon I'm back with my team.

I don't see Bombita again, but that doesn't mean I won't one day.

7

BECAUSE of his work, a cop looks at things a little different than most people. He can't help it. Sure, it would be great if all he had to deal with was an occasional traffic offense or maybe help an old lady across the street. It isn't like that, not in New York.

In New York, the cop has to deal with all the filth and dregs and sickness that nice people don't want to look at. Respectable people like to talk about how the law should be enforced and how the cop should treat everybody with respect. But they don't have to get down in the shit and fight with cruddy animals who think nothing of killing a cop.

When you're in a stinking basement with a punk who wants to cut you or kill you, your only hope is in another cop. Civilians will never understand the feeling of one cop for another, not unless they've been infantrymen and can maybe remember how they felt about the guys around them in the front line. There's an attitude like combat soldiers among cops. Like that time up in the Bronx.

A team, Detective Joe Volpe and Tommy Reilly, ask me to go and help them find a guy called Subway who's pushing stuff around Third Avenue, in the Bronx.

There'd been some complaint to City Hall that he'd been

selling to teenagers, and the boss wanted him. We go up there and I don't have much trouble spotting this Subway. I mix in with the junkies and they tell me if I want stuff, "Subway, he got stuff . . . He's over there." They point to a place on Third Avenue where it's like a department store with guys going in and coming out all the time. In the vestibule I see this guy in a gray Persian hat standing with a woman . . . Later, I find out her name is Penny. On the steam inside the vestibule is a board and on the board is junk. He's taking the money and this Penny is handing out the stuff.

Subway sees me and he says, "Come on, come on, what you sees is what you get. What d'you want?"

"Gimme three bags," I say, giving him $15. The broad hands give me three envelopes and I leave. I'm pleased. I've not only located this Subway, but I've made a buy from him. In fact, I've got two buys, because the broad can now be arrested also for acting in concert with Subway.

A few days later, I go back to Third Avenue. Don't think this is all simple. To buy from Subway, I've got to go into that hallway, and whenever I have to go into a hallway, I'm shitting. It's dangerous. The junkies going in and out are mean-looking bastards.

The hallway is full of junkies and while I'm waiting, guys tell me about a pusher called Willie, up on Davidson Avenue, who doesn't sell single bags . . . he sells loads. He'll sell maybe six decks at a time for $30, a quarter load. While we're waiting to get into Subway's hallway, we're in line, just like waiting in line at the checkout counter in a department store. Finally, I get in and make my second buy, another three bags for $15.

Back with the team, we decide to try and find this Willie who sells loads, and we go to Davidson Avenue. Willie's on the stoop of a house and I see him selling to guys, but he doesn't dig me. As I get near the stoop, I hear him say, "Hold it, here comes Whitey." He doesn't trust me one little bit, and I've got to make him trust me. I decide to show him I'm an all-right guy.

I start looking in the windows of parked cars, as if I'm looking to crack a short, so I can buy stuff. A little way away, I spot this sharp yellow auto, very neat and shiny. In the back seat, I see a couple of boxes . . . they look as if they contain suits. Now I need a wire to break in. I go to a garbage can and I find a wire clothes hanger, all the time hoping that Willie is watching. He is.

Out of the corner of my eye, I see he's watching me straightening out the clothes hanger near the yellow car.

I push the end of the wire through the crack of the door, trying to hook it around the button lock. Now Willie'll really believe I'm trying to crack a short.

But then I hear a shout, "Hey, you!" I look round and there's Willie running for me. He's shouting, "What the fuck you doing? Get away from that car!" Of course, out of all the cars on that block . . . there must have been nearly sixty, I have to choose Willie's. It's his car.

"Take it easy," I stutter. "I didn't know it was yours. I just saw a couple of suits in the back seat and . . ."

"What do you mean, you saw a couple of suits," he yells. "I'll break your fucking ass, you junkie motherfucker."

"Listen," I say. "I'm sorry. I just wanted to crack a short so I can buy some junk." It looks as though he's going to hit me, but he doesn't.

"Get the fuck off this block before I kill you," he says, and he gives me a shove and I walk off with the junkie stoop to the shoulders. I look real depressed but, really, I'm feeling pretty good because now I've convinced him I'm a junkie.

Later, I go back and I see Willie again. He's cooled off a

bit. "Look," I say, "I'm sorry about your car. If I damaged it, I'll pay you. I didn't know it was yours."

"You didn't hurt it, but you nearly did," he says.

"Hey, Willie," I say, "I'm strung out. Can you help me?"

"What d'you want?"

"I got money now," I say. "I want a couple of bundles." He sells me a quarter load and says, yeah, he'll be around if I want more. The team's pleased with my buy, especially Tommy Reilly, because it's his first experience as a member of a team.

I'd met him before when he was a patrolman on the street and I was doing some of my first undercover work in lower Manhattan. He's a strong guy, heavy arms, and a good listener. A tough cop.This time in lower Manhattan I'm making buys in a hallway with four or five junkies when this guy, Reilly, comes crashing in with his partner, both in uniform. They don't know I'm a cop. They think I'm another junkie.

They line us up at gunpoint and make us lean against the wall. I'm worried because I've got other work to do and don't want all the hassle of being taken in and wasting all that time before I can get back on the street again. If he searches me, he'll find my badge and that will make more trouble because he'll think, what's a junkie doing with a police badge?

He starts questioning me, asking my name.

"My name's Adams," I say, giving him a hard look. Now the name of the commissioner at that time was Adams. "Adams," I say again, "I live right around the corner. Why don't you call this number, Canal 6–2000?"

He looks at me peculiar, because Canal 6–2000 was the number of police headquarters. "If that doesn't do it," I go on, "call my brother at Spring 7–3100." At the time, that was the number to call for police or ambulance. Okay, he knows now. He knows that I'm an undercover cop even though I look like a mean and dirty junkie. He's a sharp guy.

Not all the cops I meet in such a situation are as sharp. A couple of them have smacked me in the face for talking like that.

One big Irishman, I tell him to call Canal 6–2000 and winked at him. He says, "What the fuck you winking at?" and he gives me a smack in the kisser. "Don't wink at me, you junkie bastard," he says. Not Tommy Reilly. He separates me from the junkies and I tell him what I have and I'm not bugged by all the hassle of being taken in.

So now Reilly is working with Joe Volpe. We decide that I'll go and make more buys. This particular place I go to is in an alleyway, full of garbage and stinking of piss. I knock on this door in the basement, standing in the garbage and dead rats and cats, and ask for Renee, who's a main pusher in the neighborhood. The smell's getting to me. A window high up above me opens and a beer can comes sailing out. More garbage.

While I'm waiting for this Renee, I start thinking about all the alleyways and basements and halls in the ghettos where I've made buys.

They weren't built to be ghettos . . . people made them into stinking slums. If people living there didn't throw their garbage out of the window, you wouldn't have slums, you wouldn't have rats and roaches and the stink of it all.

Instead of buying junk and booze, why don't these people spend three dollars on buying a can of cheap paint and a bit of plaster to fix up their places instead of screaming at their landlords? My legs are ankle-deep in garbage that people have thrown out of their windows because they can't be bothered to put it in the proper receptacle. But, I guess, a cop isn't expected to think about things like that.

Renee comes to the door . . . he's a nasty little bastard, all in black like Zorro. He tries to talk like Humphrey Bogart.

"What d'you want?" he demands. "What you bothering me for, you fucking junkie bastard?"

"Take it easy, man," I say. "Just give me three bags."

"You don't come here no more," he says. "There's a lot of trouble." I give him $15 and he slams the door on me. Shortly afterwards, another guy comes to the door and he hands me three bags. He's very cautious, worried.

"Be careful," he says, "it's very hot now. The Man's around." I know why he's worried. The narcotics division at that time is doing a bang-up job. They have good information and they have guys that really love the job—Nessie Bryant, Jimmy Ryan, Tom Clancy, Matty Chang, Joe Volpe, two black girls, Millie Jones and Pat Wyatt, Johnny Lombardo, Nick Gabriel. I could go on and on. They all know their jobs and they put the fear of God into the pushers.

They were the people who went down into greasy cellars and into dark hallways to make their buys and kick down doors to make their arrests. It's not like that today. Now you can see pushers operating openly, no longer scared.

After the buys from Renee, we wrap it up for the day. We decide we'll start to pick up the pushers on Monday, after the weekend. In the meantime, there's a party in the Red Coach Inn down in the Wall St. area for a couple of guys who are retiring and also for a detective who's being promoted to second grade. We pay for tickets, like $10 or $15 for all you can drink and a big, beautiful meal. An occasion like that, it's the one time when we can all get together, the undercover detectives and the arresting teams. It's the only time you see

126

the undercover cops dressed up properly, the men in smart suits, the girls in pretty dresses.

At a party like that, all the talk is about the job. About Tommy Lipscomb, an undercover detective who puts a pusher in jail and when the pusher comes out he finds Tommy and chases him with a German shepherd. Tommy has to jump on top of a car to get away from the dog and the pusher leaves the dog there, tied up on a long chain to the bumper, so that Tommy has to sit on top of the car for more than two hours.

About Matt O'Hara, who goes into a hallway and is mugged by three guys who take his gun. They also break his nose and rip his pants off. Matt grabs a frying pan and holds it under his nose to catch the blood, while he runs down to Lenox Avenue, trying to catch the guys who mugged him. No pants on.

About how we all get together and go back to Harlem to get back Matt O'Hara's gun. We put informers out on the street and we find the guy who has it and we retrieve it.

About Frank Beda, who goes into an apartment and then as he's coming out, he's jumped by four guys, all with guns. Frank takes his own gun and he shoots all four of them, killing three.

It's that sort of thing that puts the comradeship between cops, knowing that one day you're going to rely on the guy you're drinking with now. One day, you think, you'll walk in a hallway and there'll be a knife in your back. One day, you'll be on a rooftop or in a basement, and a lead pipe will smash into your head.

If you ask these men and women why they do it, the answer comes, "Oh, I don't know. I like the job." That's all. But there's more.

It may be a filthy job, but you know you're doing good. It gets to you. That's why we feel hurt when we hear a brother officer is in trouble because of a five-dollar bill or a free meal or something stupid like that. I go to other parties, parties where there are civilians, and I hear them talking about the cops.

A civilian, he'll say a motorcycle cop stopped him and gave him a summons and he really wasn't doing 50 m.p.h. Or, he parked in an illegal zone for only a couple of minutes and a cop gave him a ticket. Or, he gave a cop $5 or $10. Or, he sees a cop getting a free meal or a free cup of coffee. Or, around Christmastime, he sees a cop in a store getting something free as a Christmas gift.

We hear it all the time when we're among civilians. We look at each other and we just have to shrug because we can't defend cops who take. But, this is straight. The majority of us are honest. We try within the department to root out the cops who are on the take. We really do.

The public is crazy if they think policemen will stand for cops who sell drugs or use force to steal from civilians.

Any officer who does that sort of thing is not a cop any more. We don't look upon him as a cop. We clean our own house, but in the old days we didn't publicize it like they do now . . . that's the only thing I object to.

I don't believe it should be advertised as it is over the TV, radio and in the papers. What d'you think that does to the morale of the department? What do you think it does to the wives and children of honest cops who have to risk their lives —and don't mind doing it—when they find the public thinks all cops are dishonest because of all the publicity given to the few bad ones?

I still think most of the public trusts us, but that sort of

128

thing pushes cops together even more. We only have each other, nobody else. We don't make friends out of the job because our best friend is another cop.

When a cop is killed—he may be a stranger—we all go to the funeral. We're not forced to go. We go because we want to. We know, each one of us, as we look at the coffin with the flag draped on it, that it could be us.

Every time I go to a police funeral, I picture myself in the coffin. I say to myself, it's going to happen, I know it.

When I work undercover, with the silencer and with a shotgun, and certain other things I do, it's to protect myself. I'm sure other undercover men have done the same. Even the ordinary patrolman in high-crime areas, there are certain things he must do to protect himself.

If we don't take care of ourselves, nobody else is going to do it for us . . . not the judges or the lawyers. Police brutality! That's a laugh. I swear to God. That's all the public hears. You get a couple of uniformed guys in a radio car responding to a call in a high-crime area. There's a gang fight or a bunch of guys with clubs . . . you'd better believe the cop has got to punch and kick and scratch. What do you expect him to do? Advise them of their rights?

You can't do that. The street is different. The guy who wrote the book, which we're supposed to do it by, is a clerk with a pencil waving in the air. The book isn't the same as the street. Let the guy who wrote the book come out on the street and see how it works.

The New York City Police Department trains its men well. When you're in the Academy, they give you all the proper training as far as the law's concerned.

When you get onto the street, you've got to apply it but you've got to apply it in such a way that you protect yourself as well as John Q. Citizen. As I sit at this party in the Red Coach Inn, I look at all my brother officers talking and laughing around me. Each one of them has been injured in one way or another. A lot of them have the scars to prove it.

The day before, when I made the buys from Subway and Willie, those guys would kill me without hesitating for a moment and they'd enjoy doing it if they knew I was a cop. As I sit there, I know that Monday I've got to go out onto the street again and deal with guys like Subway and Willie. And the cops around me, they know that they'll have to go out and face the same sort of thing on the street.

I get so angry when I think about it. Every day in the New York City Police Department, we get orders, what they call TOPs and SOPs, how to behave, how to act to the public. Our supervisors, our commissioner, they constantly tell us to do this and do that, and, believe me, we try. We really do.

Our supervisors, they all mean well. But there are some of these orders that cannot be applied in the street. They cannot. In these high-crime areas where they're constantly yelling about police brutality . . . police brutality, hell. We're dealing with brutal people and brutal situations.

Every time a cop defends himself, it's police brutality. It's about time the people who live on Park Avenue and who go on about police brutality came down to see what the ordinary cop has to deal with . . . on behalf of those same people on Park Avenue.

Me, I can't afford to live on Park Avenue. The best I can manage is a home out in the suburbs, and there are those who say my family shouldn't be there. They say we should live in the city because we're cops in the city.

Well, I have a right to live in the suburbs. Don't I have

a constitutional right to live where I want? How can I subject my family to city life? I know what the city is because I'm a street man and I don't want my kids to walk that street. Every day, I see the shit and the violence and I've worked hard and risked my life and been injured so that my kids don't have to live in it.

Law and order . . . it's become a joke phrase. But I don't care. I'm a law and order man because that's my life, and it's the life of the men and women at the party who risk their lives to enforce it.

Monday, we go up to the Bronx, the team and me. I'm wearing a dark brown fedora with hair sticking out at the side. I haven't shaved.

I've got on a black corduroy shirt that Helen bought at Alexander's for three bucks, an oil-stained dark blue zippered jacket, dark brown pants and scuffed-up old shoes. I've got my revolver. I stripped down the butt and taped it so that it would lie flat against my belly inside my shorts.

First, I make my second buy from Willie . . . three bags for $15. Then I double up on Renee, the guy in the basement down the garbage-strewn ally . . . one bag for $5.

Subway comes next. We decide that I'll go looking for him on Third Avenue and when I've found where he is, I'll go back to the team and tell them so they can make the collar. I start looking in hallways and checking with local junkies.

"He's somewhere around," one junkie says. "You know Subway, he walk around, he keep moving to fool The Man."

I go on looking. I don't know it at the time, but Tommy Reilly is behind me at a distance all this time. I never did find out why he didn't follow our plan.

In this one vestibule . . . all broken mailboxes and garbage and scribbling on the walls . . . I give a whistle.

131

A voice comes from a room on the ground floor. "Who whistling?" it says. "You don't have to whistle. Come on in, man."

It's Subway. He's in a room with his broad Penny and two others. One is a guy, at least 6 feet 2 inches, and 180 pounds, and the other is a woman. On top of the radiator is a three-foot-long board on which are piles of money and junk. They're packaging the stuff.

"What d'you want?" Subway says. "What you see is what you get."

"Is this the same stuff I got last time?"

"Yeah," Subway says, "it's the same stuff. Where's your bread?" The second broad puts out her hand and I stick $10 in it. The tall dude . . . his name is Forrest . . . he hands me two decks.

Just as he's doing that, I hear a crashing down of the door and who the hell comes in but Tommy Reilly. I don't want this. I don't want to be there when they arrest Subway and Penny. I'm shook. Reilly orders us up against the wall. He's got his gun out. Subway and Forrest and the two girls and me, we all turn and put our hands up against the wall. I'm wondering what happened to Joe Volpe.

Tommy is questioning one of the broads and at the same time picking up the stuff and the money from the board. Subway is leaning against the wall next to me and now he starts whispering to me.

"Listen close," he mutters. "When I make my move, you're gonna help me, baby. You understand?"

I don't like the way this is going, not one little bit.

"What're you talking about?" I whisper back.

"I'm gonna stab this motherfucker," Subway says. "When I stab him, I want you to grab him. You gonna help me. Unnerstand?"

Oh, shit, I think. How the hell am I going to get out of this? I tell him, "Subway. I don't want no problems. Please, man, I'm clean. Let's just take the bust . . ."

"Get this," he whispers. "Listen to me, white mother-fucker. We're gonna get this guy. They want me down in South Carolina. I killed a sheriff down there. They're not taking me in."

I see him reach down slowly and pull out a knife. The handle alone is about 10 inches long. Altogether, when it's open it's about 18 inches. Here I am in a hallway with a killer who wants to cut up a cop, and if I don't help, he'll cut my throat too.

"Subway," I plead, "it doesn't pay to try it. The Man's got us. There's gotta be more guys on the outside."

"Do it," he says. "When he comes behind me, you grab him or I'll cut your gut. I'll snatch his gun and I'll cut him." Reilly doesn't hear any of this. Where the fuck is Joe Volpe? I know Subway is going to do it. His body is between his blade and Reilly, but I can see him gripping it and for sure he's going to do it.

There's only one thing I can do. I step back from the wall. I say to Subway, "Forget it, Subway. I'm The Man. I'm a cop, Subway." And I reach into my shirt where I've got my badge hanging on a chain and I pull it out and show it to him. I tell him the whole thing, that I'm an undercover man making buys so the team can come in and make the collar, that now it's the two of us against him and Forrest and the two broads.

He can't believe it. He stares at me and he stares at my badge. Now I know just how much I fooled him. He starts getting excited.

"You rat," he says. "You motherfucking rat. You ain't a cop. You a rat. You like that sheriff." He's getting more and more excited. Tommy Reilly's got his hands full. The other three are beginning to move, getting excited like Subway. This guy Forrest, he's enormous and Tommy Reilly's pretty short . . . he only just made the cops.

I reach into my groin and I pull out my gun. I point it at Subway. "Listen to me, Subway," I say, "I'm a cop. Don't make me blow you away."

"You ain't a cop . . . you a rat," he keeps on saying. He's still got the knife. Suddenly, everything goes mad. Tommy Reilly fires a shot and there's screams and yelling. Forrest and the two broads have jumped him.

Subway comes at me with his blade. He lunges for my face but I step back and the blade catches me down the chest. The knife slices through my jacket and my shirt so that they fall apart, exposing my chest. It even cuts through my T-shirt, but it doesn't touch my skin. Not even a graze. Freaky.

Then Subway punches me, sending me reeling back, and he comes after me until we're grappling and fighting. I've still got my gun in my hand. I don't want to fire it, believe me. It's tough to shoot a guy.

Another shot. Tommy Reilly's got his hands full. Forrest and the two broads have him on the ground underneath them, but he's fighting all three of them.

I kick Subway and send him back against the wall, but he's ready to come at me again.

"Drop that knife," I shout. "You know I'm a cop. Now drop it. Don't make me shoot you, Subway!"

His face is wild, all shiny with sweat. He's scaring the hell out of me. My gun is pointed right at him and when he starts coming for me again, I know I have to blow him away. I don't want to kill the bastard. I lower my gun and I fire a shot. The bullet blows his balls away. He doesn't make a sound. He stops. He stares at me. He drops the knife and he holds his groin. And then, as he's going down, he looks up and he throws himself forward at me.

He brings me down with him and he tries to get me round the throat, but he has no strength. He's bleeding bad . . . there's a lot of blood now. I'm more worried about Tommy Reilly. As I look over towards him, I see this giant Forrest get up and start running. He takes a flying leap over Subway, whose belly is pouring blood, and me and he crashes right through the glass panels and wood of the vestibule door. Everything shatters and splinters and then Forrest is through and in the street and he's running.

I pull myself clear of Subway, who's moaning and groaning on the floor, and with my gun in my hand I start running after this Forrest. When I get to the street, I see him half a block away and I go after him. That's when Joe Volpe shows up.

What had happened was this: Reilly had come in after me, thinking Joe would be close behind. But Joe was parking the car and when he'd done that, he found that both me and Reilly had disappeared off the block. By then we were inside with Subway and Forrest and the two broads. Joe starts looking for us, driving up and down the block, honking his horn.

The next thing he sees is this guy Forrest come flying into the street and then me with my gun in my hand. I catch up with Forrest and I make a flying tackle, bringing him to the ground.

We're wrestling and I lash him across the face with my gun. "I give up," he yells, "I give up." He's got blood on his face now.

That's when Joe Volpe catches up with us in his car. He

drives right up onto the sidewalk and nearly runs us down, he's so excited. The car hits a couple of trash cans and I have to roll away to dodge his right front wheel, which is coming right for me.

Joe jumps out of his car and I say, "Okay, Joe, everything is okay." He says, "Bullshit," and he gives Forrest a punch. Then he cuffs the guy and we walk him back to the hallway.

Tommy Reilly comes running out, huffing and puffing. He's got one of the girls, Penny, but the other woman has run off into the backyard. I go after her.

I'm searching the backyards and soon some patrolmen turn up to help. After a bit, I get onto a foundation wall and I spot some red through the fences. This broad's wearing a red coat. There's a patrolman near her, although he hasn't seen her, and I point her out to him. He and the other cops grab her and when I turn up, still with gun in hand, they've got her cuffed.

An ambulance rolls up and as Subway is getting in, he sees me. "That's the guy who shot me," he yells. "That's him." He still doesn't believe I'm a cop . . . The guy still doesn't believe me.

Now the formalities start. You wouldn't believe what a cop has to go through when he fires his gun. I'm interviewed by sergeants, lieutenants, captains and an inspector. It goes on for hours. I call Helen eventually and tell her I'm coming home.

"They kept you late again," she says. "Never mind. I'll have some food ready. But, listen, Tony, before you come home, pick up two quarts of milk and a loaf of bread. And, Tony, will you go to Korvette's and pick up some underwear for the children, size six?"

I don't tell her about the fight because there's no point in

136

worrying her. I tell Helen okay, and I drive to a shopping center near home. I pick up the milk and the bread and I go into Korvette's. I'm unshaven, in old clothes, with hair all over my face. . . . I look like a real bum.

I hear the snapping of fingers and out of the corner of my eye I see all the security men in Korvette's pointing at me and watching me. They're sure I'm a down-and-out on a shoplifting expedition. I ignore them. After picking up the underwear, I put my hand in my pocket to take out my money to pay for it. To reach my money, I have to take out the dope I've bought in the paper bag. All of a sudden, the bag breaks and all the glassine envelopes full of narcotics spill out over the floor.

They know they've got a dope fiend. The security men jump on me, grabbing my arms and pulling them behind me. They pick up the envelopes and drag me off to a private office. Man, am I pissed off.

When they search me further and find my gun, they get very upset and very excited. They call the police and while we're waiting, they question me. But I'm pissed off plenty now. I won't talk to them.

One of the security men says, "Yeah, I know this guy. He was in here last week. He's the guy who took all the perfume from the perfume case."

Another says, "Yeah, and he's the one who took that small TV set the other day." They're trying to pin everything on me. The door opens and I see a crowd gathered outside. In comes a tall patrolman. He sees the gun on a table and the narcotics. He thinks he's got a good arrest here.

I tell the cop I want to talk to him privately. He's reluctant because he thinks I'm going to give him trouble, but I convince him and all the store people step out of the office. When we're all alone, I reach inside my shirt and I pull out my gold shield. He doesn't believe me . . . he thinks I stole it. But then I start talking about other cops who live in the area, cops he knows. I tell him that I'm undercover for the Narcotics Bureau.

"What's the number of the Narcotics Bureau?" he wants to know. I tell him, and he calls them. They verify my story. I then have him call another cop at home, a guy we both know. Finally, he's satisfied. He hands me the evidence and my gun before calling in the security men.

They're all smiling. "We're gonna book him on that other stuff he took," one of them says.

The patrolman says, "No, we're not. We're going to free him. He's a cop." They don't want to, but they have to let me go. I drive home.

Later on, the department decides to give me a medal, a commendation. Subway goes to jail, but he gets parole and while he's still on parole, he dies. When I hear about this, I'm very depressed because I think he died as a result of the wounds . . . because of me shooting his balls off. I check into it and I find he died from an overdose of heroin.

138

8

HELEN is a quiet woman. I guess you could say a Victorian kind of woman. She doesn't particularly like going out. She's happy in her home with our kids. That's the way she was brought up. Even though she's a pretty American housewife, living in a split-level suburban house, some of her Italian background remains. And that means my word is law around the house. Well, mostly.

She doesn't agree with me on some things. Like, she's against the death penalty and I'm not. She thinks the guy who gets arrested should be given a break. I try to tell her it's crazy to coddle a criminal but she says, "If they coddle a thousand criminals and just one is rehabilitated, then it's worth it." She has a mind of her own, and like anybody else we have our disagreements.

Sometimes my job comes into it. Like the time when her sister was dying in a hospital and she wanted me to drive her over there. But I had a meet set up with Clancy and Chang to make arrests and I told Helen I couldn't do what she wanted. She was upset but, even so, she settled the argument before I left the house, even apologizing. When I was undercover, she made a point of sending me out of the house with an easy mind. She didn't want me working on the street, dealing with killers and muggers and pushers, worrying all the time about something at home.

She knew that a distraction like that could screw me up bad. In my job, I needed all my concentration on the work at hand. In this case, when Helen finally got to the hospital, her sister was dead. I feel lousy about it to this day.

She never said much about how she felt towards my police work, how she felt when I was undercover, getting hurt in dirty alleys and stinking hallways. She knew I was always in danger when I was on the street.

On the surface, at least, she accepted it, but there was one time when she got really angry. I never saw her like that before.

She didn't mind so much that detective teams would call up and ask when I was available to work with them, although some of them were rude as hell, demanding to know where I was and which team I was working with at the time.

Because I spent all my time in the street, these detectives could only reach me at home and sometimes they treated Helen like a secretary. This one time, a detective and his wife, they call up and invite us to dinner, Helen and me and the kids. They're real insistent.

"I'm dying to meet you," this detective's wife tells Helen. "You must come. I've heard so much about Tony and you. You must come this Sunday." She makes a big thing out of it and Helen, she doesn't want to go but she can't refuse. She can't understand why this wife is going on and on, pleading with her to come. Finally, she says okay.

On the day, there's a snowstorm and Helen calls them to put it off but this wife, she absolutely insists. She says the snow's not bad and everything's prepared. We have to go.

Before we sit down to this tremendous dinner, the detective takes out his diary and starts booking me for future undercover work, this date and that date, this area and that area. He books me for work months in advance. I can't refuse, not in his home with dinner waiting.

I can tell Helen's upset about something, but we have the dinner and we talk and finally we leave. The moment we're out of the door, Helen lets me have it.

"Tony," she says, "that detective . . . he invited us to dinner so he could get hold of you and get you to work with him. Do you realize he booked you up for months in advance. And he used me and the kids, inviting us up for dinner, just so he could get hold of you when you couldn't refuse. He used us and I don't like that."

Jesus, she was mad, and suddenly I realized she was right. That sonofabitch didn't want to meet Helen and the kids. He just wanted to book me and he put on this dinner with his wife calling up so that he could get plenty of arrests in the future. Screw him. But I still went out and worked with him.

There were other problems at home. Helen says that since I've been working on the street with these addicts, these animals . . . some of it's rubbed off on me. My language. I was never a prissy talker but now, even at home, the obscenities and the swearing and the street language come out. You can't help it, when you're spending more than half your life in that work with junkies who swear with every other word and sometimes in the middle of the word. If you don't use their language, you draw attention, and that's the last thing an undercover guy wants.

At home, if I use that language, I feel bad immediately and I apologize, but the words are out. Helen doesn't like it but she understands how it comes about. That's the thing about Helen, she understands. One good thing, half the swearing

I use around the house is in Spanish and she doesn't know Spanish, so it's not so bad. Even then, though, she knows it's not drawing room stuff.

She put up with more than that. When I was undercover, I'd always wear dirty old clothes and my hair would be long and all over the place and I'd be unshaven. No bargain. She didn't like it, but she understood why it had to be.

Helen used to ask her family for old clothes they were throwing out so that I could use them on the street. Once I gave her hell. I found her ironing one of my shirts that I needed for the street. She spent 45 minutes pressing the damned thing. It was neat enough for an insurance office, and the places I was heading for weren't insurance offices. I had to grab it and crumple it and throw it around and step on it until it looked bad enough for the street.

Then there were the few times we could manage to go shopping together, me straight from the streets in my dirty old clothes. I guess we looked strange, Helen dressed nice and me looking like a bum. The store detectives used to follow us around, sure we were shoplifting. If we went to a restaurant, the waiters would look queer at us and wouldn't serve us at first, hoping we'd leave. They didn't want us in their place.

It bothered me, not for myself, but that Helen should be embarrassed like that, and we didn't do it much. She said she didn't mind, that she was proud of me, whatever I wore, but it still got to me.

We had some nosy neighbors in one building we lived in and one of them came right out and asked Helen what I did, how come I always looked so lousy, why I was never home. Helen can be tough when she wants. She told this woman it was none of her business.

Helen couldn't make friends outside cop families because

142

she didn't want people in the neighborhood to know what I did. We were living in the Bronx, where I was buying narcotics, and Helen was scared that if word got around that I was a cop, it might be dangerous for me on the street.

She decided, in fact, that the fewer friends we had, the safer I'd be. That's some way for a woman to live . . . but she did it.

Always, when I was out on the street, she would wait dinner for me, as long as possible. Many nights, she'd fall asleep sitting at the kitchen table waiting for me. She'd wake up and I'd still not be home and, of course, she'd be worrying.

Once or twice, she's let her feelings slip. She'd say how frightened she was for me, but usually she kept it hidden. She says it had an effect on her personality, making her calmer and more understanding once she adjusted to knowing I had a dangerous job and there was nothing she could do about it.

Once she told me, "Tony, you've chosen this hazardous work and every minute that we're together is very important to me and I'm not going to spend any of that time arguing or fighting over small things. It's too precious for that." It got to me, that did.

There were good things. She liked my friends, most of them undercover men like me, or arresting officers. Helen said they were all like me, energetic, aggressive. She got on well with their wives because they had the same sort of problems she had. Like holidays, it didn't matter whether it was Christmas, Easter or Thanksgiving, none of the wives could be sure their husbands would be around. They just had to do their best to make the holidays nice for the children without their husbands.

Helen was happy, also, when I made first grade detective.

It meant extra money for the household but, more than that, she knew how pleased I was that I got promoted. She only had to look at my face to see I was busting with it. Afterwards, she said to me, "You know, Tony, the only time I saw you happier was when I gave birth to the children."

The money, well, Helen's not a spender, although she likes nice things around her. She's a homebody . . . she wouldn't mind if she never left the house.

She was happiest of all, though, when they pulled me out of the narcotics division after nine years. I didn't want to leave . . . I was used to it and it was home for me. But Helen, she was tickled pink. She was glad I was getting into something that wasn't so dangerous, not so dirty, where I would be a proper detective with a partner. She would know what my hours were, instead of never being sure when I would come home. It meant she could prepare meals and have some hope I'd be there to eat them.

And now I could look the way she wanted me to look— like a real detective in clean clothes. It meant we needed that extra money because I had to buy decent clothes instead of spending all my time in shabby old things. I never used to buy good clothes because I could hardly ever wear them. She told me how good she felt to see me leaving the house clean-shaven and neat.

The nightmares, though, they still wake her up. She tells me I tremble in my sleep and make motions as if I'm running, trying to get away from somebody. And she doesn't like to see the scar of the stab mark on my back when I take my shirt off. It reminds her of the days in undercover.

She told me once she'd have been perfectly happy if I'd remained an ordinary patrolman, because then I wouldn't have caused her so much worry.

Part of it was the phone calls she sometimes got, saying I was wounded, or once telling her I was dead. She told me she refused to believe the calls were about me. She would say to herself, "That's not my Tony. That's somebody else it happened to."

The other thing was that she felt some of the detectives talked down to me because I was dirty and wore old clothes. When the teams would call me up, they would talk rough to her, demanding to know who I was working with and where I was, as if she was some kind of servant. She put them right about that. She didn't like it that they got the glory of all the arrests while I was in a more dangerous position but never made the collars. Sometimes these guys would call up at two or three in the morning, waking up our kids. It wasn't easy for her.

She put up with it because she knew I wanted to do the work, that it gave me a sense of accomplishment. But it didn't help her peace of mind any. She says she won't have that until I retire from the police.

As for me, when I was undercover, I couldn't relax like other guys, sitting in an armchair and that sort of thing.

There was a way, though. I'd wait for a nice sunny day and then I'd drive out to Teterboro airport and rent a plane. The tension in my body would start to go as soon as I smelled the fresh air around the airstrip and the oil from the aircraft.

I would settle in the plane and off I'd go down the runway and head north over the Catskills. No special destination. I'd just fly. At 5,000 feet, I'd level off and trim the craft. The plane just floated there and I'd listen to the drone of the engine. It was so calm. I could feel my bones relaxing. No more houses, no more tenements, no more dirty hallways, no more garbage-littered streets. No more fear. I'd forget the

145

ghost faces of the pushers and junkies . . . Subway and Sonny and Bobby Bombita.

It was as good as a night's sleep. Because I didn't get good sleep. Not after that time they tried to kill me on Staten Island. I'd wake up in the middle of the night, sometimes screaming, soaked in sweat. When I came down from the sky, I'd be refreshed, ready to go back to Harlem and the Bowery and the South Bronx.

There was another way. Parachuting. That's real boss. After a jump, I'd be ready to go back to the streets.

There was a third way I could get the same sort of feeling as flying and parachuting and it didn't cost so much. I first went up into the backwoods when I was in a Boy Scout troop in East Harlem. For me, knowing only tenements and asphalt, it was a revelation, the trees and the wild things and the quiet.

While I was a young patrolman, I started saving, putting spare money in a milk bottle. When it was full, I broke it and took the money and bought back-packing equipment . . . the good, elaborate stuff that mountain climbers use. I joined a back-packing club. And, later, when I was undercover, that's how I would get away from all the violence and the shit.

I trekked into the wilderness and smelled the good air and saw all the beauty and I would lie down and go to sleep under the stars. When I was up there, I could really sleep—deep exhausted good sleep. I fitted up my boys, Mark and Anthony, with back-pack gear.

We started going into the foothills of the Catskills together. I taught them about the woods . . . how to make a fire, I pointed out various plants, showed them how to prepare a camp and how to leave everything as clean as they found it. They loved it. As I used to watch them, I thought,

146

this is real relaxation, not lying in a soft bed somewhere with locked doors, wondering if a burglar's trying to get in to steal and feed his habit.

Once again, I could forget about the pushers, Lynch and Frankie Conte from Staten Island and Bubba from Amsterdam Avenue. But, this one time, I learn you can't escape.

We're on a hike and I'm watching my boys bedding down and then I look up at the stars in the black sky and I drift off to sleep. I'm the type of guy, though, who immediately comes awake if there's the slightest unusual noise. It happens now. I'm suddenly awake and I can hear a rustling that's different to the normal noises in the woods. I'm not worried. In fact, I'm smiling.

Every so often, you'll get animals foraging in the garbage pit which we always dig, and that's what I think it is. Deer, maybe. I put my head back on the ground and go to sleep again. The next morning, we break camp, covering the garbage hole with dirt so the place looks the same as it did when we arrived. I tell Mark and Anthony that the code of the wilderness is that the only trace you leave behind is footprints.

But as we are putting our stuff back in our packs, I notice some things are missing, like some food, utensils, a lantern, a small stove, an ax and a flashlight. I get angry with my boys because the items are missing from their packs. I tell them they should take care of things, not lose them like that.

"Dad," Anthony says, "we didn't lose those things. We had them. I remember seeing them before we went to bed." I pay them no mind, and off we go along the trail. As we're going along, I'm thinking about the ghetto. Watching my boys, I think back to the kids I've dealt with in the slums and what they're missing. They don't have to miss it. It doesn't

147

cost money. Even a dishwasher could take a $5 bill for the bus fare and a couple of boloney sandwiches and he could get his kids and take them on a bus going upstate to Bear Mountain.

They could leave the bus and right there, they'd be on the trails and the guy could show his children there's something worthwhile in the world, something more than the tenements and the stinking streets. Even a person on welfare could do it.

Our destination is Island Pond, north of the Harriman State Park at the foot of the Catskills. It's beautiful. The shores are covered with bright green shrubbery and pine trees and high rocks. The lake is about a mile by a mile and a half, with plenty of fish in it. Trout, bass, pickerel, anything you want.

We make camp on a little plateau, about twenty-five feet above the surface of the lake. The boys want to fish and they take out their rods and settle down at the edge of the water. "Daddy," calls Mark, "look at the water. Look at the fish!"

He's seen a fish jump out of the water to catch an insect and I can see the ripple where the fish was. I look out and I can see a series of rings all over the lake where the fish are jumping.

The water, except for the ripples, is smooth as plastic. No wind. It's sundown, the last rays streaming through the tree branches. I think, wow! What more could anybody want? A street man like me, he can't express himself the way an educated man can. The words, they're not there. All I can say is that this is beauty. As I sit, my back against a rock, watching my two little boys, I'm happy. Mark's got a couple of nibbles, and the expression on his face, that's better than any junkie high could be.

148

The darkness starts moving in and still we sit there in the quiet. The boys fishing. Me thinking. Now the city jungle is far away.

But I'm wrong. The jungle follows me. I hear a sound, a sort of "whoop . . . whoop." Mark turns and he says, "Daddy, that sounds like an owl." Anthony chips in, "Yeah, it's an owl, somewhere over there." Sure, it does sound like an owl, but to me it sounds like a phony owl, somebody imitating one. A bit later, we hear it again, and now I become suspicious. I look towards the sound and I see a head duck down behind a large boulder at the edge of the pines, behind me

It's instinctive. I reach into my waistband and I pull out my 25 caliber automatic. I carry that piece with me when I go flying, fishing, camping, anywhere. Because you find animals everywhere, and I don't mean the kind that walk on four legs. I don't need a gun to handle animals that walk on four legs.

I'm pissed off. Here I am in the woods with my boys and suddenly I've got a gun in my hand and I'm back on the street.

Very quietly, I say, "Anthony, Mark, put away your fishing rods please." They're enjoying themselves and they haven't seen the head behind us. "Aw, Dad," they protest. I speak more seriously. "Do what I tell you. Now." They look at me and see the expression on my face. They know I mean what I'm saying. They know something's wrong and they pull in their lines and put their rods on the ground.

"Listen to me," I say, still quiet. "Start to pick up firewood. But don't leave this immediate area. Put the wood in a pile and stay with it." Good kids that they are, they obey me. I move to my left until I'm out of view of anybody on

149

the slope above us. When I'm clear, I crawl away to the rear of the knoll on which I see the head. A few minutes later, through the brush, I see two heads bobbing up and down. They're making strange noises, as if to attract attention.

As I get nearer, I see they're lying on their bellies looking down at the plateau where my boys are. They're unruly-looking, with filthy clothes and matted hair. Behind them, they've got a couple of blankets laid out, and on the blankets their gear is strewn about. I break the brushline and while I'm walking towards them, very quiet, what do I see but some of my missing food on the blankets. My gas stove. My flashlight. My lantern. And in the hand of one of the guys is my ax.

These lousy sonsofbitches . . . they've brought their stinking thievery up from the city to this beautiful wilderness. They're fucking up the one place where I try to forget all that shit. I'm pissed off. I think, they're making those noises to try and draw us away, and then one of them will slip down and steal some more. Over their heads, I can see my boys looking up, trying to make out where the noises are coming from.

My automatic is cocked. I point it at them and I say, "Hey, scum!" The two of them immediately look around and they jump to their feet. The guy with the ax has it half raised. I keep my gun on them.

"What the hell are you doing?" I say. "What's going on?"

"Man, we're just camping," one of them says. "We're sleeping out."

"What's that in your hand?"

"That's my ax, man."

"That's not your ax," I say. "You lousy bastards. You stole that ax from me. You been following us, stealing our gear."

This one guy, in a short suede jacket and torn jeans, he smiles. When he does that, I can't help myself. I'm back in the South Bronx and Harlem and the Lower East Side. I clench my left fist and I give him a short left hook, catching him right on the cheekbone. He goes down. The other guy, the one with the ax, backs off to the edge of the drop down to the plateau where my boys are.

"Drop the ax," I say.

"Man, take it easy!"

"Drop the ax." He won't. I kick him in the belly. He totters back and falls down the slope. The ax goes off into the brush. I pull the guy I punched to his feet by his collar and I put my gun to his ear, then I take him down to the other guy. The man below had hurt his backside.

"Help your friend up," I say. "Pick up your blankets, leave my stuff where it is. Get on that trail and head back to the highway." They're very obedient now. They don't say anything. They just go back up and pick up their blankets. "Get going," I say. "I'm gonna be right behind you." They take off, almost at a run, down the trail.

My boys are huddled together, very scared by what has happened. I explain what it's all about and tell them to pack up. By now, it's very dark. I want to get away . . . our expedition has been wrecked by these two fucks. We slip our packs onto our shoulders and we start to walk out of the woods, back to the highway. We don't say much.

9

COLORED balloons. Kid stuff, right? Not always. When I was undercover, I learned what you can do with an ordinary colored balloon. It began when a narco back-up team, Detectives Joe Anthony and Sid Lamb, operating on the Lower East Side, wanted an undercover man to work with them. They asked for me.

This Joe Anthony, he looked like a movie star, but he talked even worse than me. Real Brooklyn stuff . . . dese, dem and dose. He knew me because he was once undercover himself and I broke him in. He didn't like the work and he became an arresting officer, teamed up with Lamb.

This area they want me in is the East Village and the Bowery. It's as bad as any in the city for junk. Working with Anthony and Lamb, I make buys from eight heroin pushers. Then I come across a guy called Sonny, about 23 and at least 6 feet 2 inches. He's the unluckiest pusher I ever meet. A real loser.

He's always losing his stuff. Either the cops grab him, search him and find the junk or else the junkies mug him and take his supply. No matter how he hides the heroin . . . in his shoes, in his underwear . . . the cops always find it.

He thinks up a plan.

He goes uptown and he steals an English racing bicycle. Now, he thinks, he's got mobility. He can escape from junkies who want to mug him by riding off very fast on his racer. Or, if the cops try to make a collar, he can ride up a one-way street against the traffic so the cops can't follow him in their car.

I'm on Avenue C making my buys, and I see this guy tearing around on his bicycle. He's a fixture in the neighborhood, selling his junk, and then racing off to his next customer. This one day, I see him on his racer and he's got a lot of colored balloons. He's got them tied to his handlebars.

That's a switch, I think, a pusher who likes colored balloons. He's doing a pretty good business. Kids buy the balloons from him as well. I keep watching. I notice that guys I know as junkies are buying these damned balloons. They're walking around with the string in their hand and a balloon floating, all nice and pretty, over their freaked-out heads.

The next day, I'm hanging around in my beat-up clothes and my hairy face with the stoop to my shoulders when I see Sonny again. He's still got the balloons tied to his bike—red, blue and green.

He doesn't know me as a junkie yet and he's real leery, so I don't approach him. Instead, I go back to my team and I tell them about this pusher who likes balloons. I tell them they'd better check him out.

Joe Anthony and Lamb drive around until they spot him on a street corner. He looks like a legitimate balloon salesman. As soon as he sees the team pull up, he unties the balloons from the handlebars of his bike and lets them go. They float up into the blue sky. A dozen of these different-colored balloons going up and up. They look real pretty.

The team searches this Sonny, but they don't find anything

except some rubber bands and some deflated balloons in his pockets. Finally, they have to leave him and walk away and he looks after them with a big grin on his puss. He gets on his bike and off he pedals as hard as he can. He's got to be a healthy guy with all the exercise he gets on that bike.

Every time the team picks up a junkie or a pusher, Anthony and Lamb ask them about Sonny and they say, yeah, sure he's pushing dope. By now, my operation is just about finished, but I'm still tickled by this guy Sonny and his balloons.

Once again I'm standing on Avenue C with some junkies talking about copping some stuff, when along comes Sonny with his English racer. This afterbirth, he's got about ten colored balloons this time.

One of the junkies I'm with says, "Hey, there's Sonny . . . I'm gonna cop now."

"You gonna cop from Sonny?" I say.

"Yeah, he's got good stuff." Okay, here we go. I feel for my money, the fives on one side, the ones on the other. Sonny sees the junkies and he stops. He looks as if he just came from a circus with all those fucking balloons. We go over to him. He seems real nervous.

"What youse want?" he says.

I say, "What you got?"

"Six-dollar bags," he says. "Are you shooting up with them?" Now I know he's leery. He wants to be sure I'm with the junkies.

"Nah," I say, "I'm picking up for myself and two other guys. Give me three bags." He looks around for a moment, then he says, "Gimme $18." I give him the money and he gives me three balloons, all red.

As I walk away, with those balloons floating over my head,

154

I'm feeling pretty ridiculous, paying $18 for three balloons and now I've got to walk around with them. After a while, I know I'm being followed. I know it. I look around and spot three guys coming after me. I cross the street and look back and, yeah, they've crossed too. I cross again and they also cross. I'm getting upset.

They're going to take me off before I can get to my team which is waiting for me on 14th Street. I'm pretty sure it's the balloons they're after, but I want to keep my balloons.

Just then a bus comes along and stops a few yards from me. Immediately, I jump on board but the driver says, "You can't come on this bus with those balloons."

I say, "Sir, why can't I come on with my balloons? Is there a regulation?"

The real reason he doesn't want me is that I look like a bum and he thinks that a guy like me with those balloons must be some kind of a wacko. I pay my fare, and I convince him I'm taking the balloons home to my kids. By the time I've finished telling him about my kids, he's almost in tears. Two or three stops further on, I get off and go to my team.

"What the hell you got there?" Lamb says.

"Balloons," I say. "I paid $18 for them."

"You got taken, you stupid fuck," Anthony growls. "You boid brain."

I'm busy popping the balloons and pulling the rubber apart. In each one, of course, I find a glassine envelope and there's stuff in each envelope. A clever fuck, this Sonny.

What he does is, he puts six dollar bags in the red balloons, three-dollar bags in the blue balloons and nothing in the green balloons. When kids want to buy balloons, he sells the green ones to them for a quarter.

Sid Lamb says, "When we saw you buy the balloons, we

couldn't see who you bought them from. We thought you were having some fun. Why don't you go back and make your second buy?"

I go back and I'm waiting on the corner of Avenue C and Fifth Street with a couple of junkies when this nut on the bicycle rides by. He's going at breakneck speed and he's got those freaking balloons attached to his bike.

I whistle at him to stop him and he wheels around to me. "What d'you want," he says, "red balloon or blue balloon?"

"Gimme a blue one," I say and give him $3. He tears off and I start walking back to my team on 14th Street. Once again, I get this feeling I'm being followed. Back of me are the same three guys who followed me before and I walk faster, but it's no good. They catch up to me. They surround me and one of them says, "Gimme the balloon." They have their hands in their pockets and I'm thinking they've got blades in there. Shit, I think, I can always buy another balloon, and I give this guy the string attached to the blue balloon.

One of the other guys says, "Okay, now empty out your pockets." Bullshit, I think. I don't mind giving them the balloon, but they're not taking me off for my money. I make believe I'm going to empty my pockets, but instead I throw a front snapkick at the guy in front of me. He reels back, but I slip onto my knee and I injure my kneecap. The other two guys take off, running, and I get up and run the opposite way.

Now I know what these guys do. They follow junkies who've bought from Sonny and they hold them up for their balloons so they can get the junk and shoot up. Every time they see a junkie with a balloon floating over his head, they know they've got a bag of dope. They even know whether it's a three-dollar bag or a six-dollar bag because the balloon is like a moving advertisement.

A couple of days later, after my knee has healed, we go back to make the second buy from Sonny. I don't know what happened to the blue balloon the three guys snatched from me . . . maybe it just floated away in the confusion of the fight. Again I'm hanging around Avenue C with some junkies and again I see Sonny pedaling furiously around the neighborhood. This time he doesn't have any balloons.

One of the junkies stops him, gives him some money and Sonny races off as if he's taking part in that French bicycle race.

"What gives?" I ask.

"Sonny's gone to get my stuff for me," the junkie says, and a few minutes later Sonny shows up, but he's still got no balloons. He stops at the curb, looks at the junkie and then spits something out onto the sidewalk . . . something red and shiny. The junkie picks it up and Sonny pedals away. It's a deflated red balloon and inside is the deck the junkie has paid for. The junkie puts the wet rubber containing the deck in his mouth and he walks away.

After a while, Sonny pedals by again and this time I stop him. He's been pedaling so fast he's panting. "What d'you want?" he says, all out of breath.

"Gimme three six-dollar bags," I say. I give him $18 and he tells me to wait where I am. A bit later, up comes Sonny and he spits out three rubbers at me. I know why he and the junkies are carrying the deflated balloons and the stuff in their mouths. If a cop stops them, they can swallow it because the smooth rubber goes down the throat easily without making you gag.

When the cops have gone, the junkie can stick a finger

down his throat and puke out the balloon, or a day later he can recover it from the toilet bowl when he has a crap.

When the dope is inside the rubber, it won't dissolve, so it comes out as good as new, untouched. That's why sometimes a cop will jump out of his car and immediately punch or slap a pusher, or grab him by the throat to stop him swallowing. An onlooker will say that's police brutality, but it's not.

I've doubled up on the guy, so I tell the team it's time to arrest him before some patrolman grabs him for selling balloons without a permit. Suddenly, as we're deciding this, here he comes, pedaling furiously with three balloons floating above his head. Leaving the team quickly, I go to the corner and whistle at him, but he pays no mind. He keeps going, so the team starts after him with a burning of rubber. I think, now they've got him. But a few minutes later, here comes the balloon man again, pedaling as hard as ever. He makes a hurried delivery to a junkie near me and then he whisks away again. After he's gone, the team rolls up looking puzzled. They've lost him.

I can't tell them where he's gone because there are other junkies around me. Raising my hand while the team's watching me, I scratch my head, and while I'm doing this I point with my thumb to show them which way he went. They zap off again and a moment later who appears but the balloon man coming from the opposite direction.

He goes whizzing south on Avenue C. I whistle at him and shout, "Hey, Sonny!" He doesn't stop, but he indicates that I should stay where I am and he'll be back. Back comes the team, staring at me in puzzlement again. Once more, I scratch my head, pointing with my thumb and off they go, wheels spinning.

158

This is getting ridiculous, I think. The team's out of sight and Sonny appears again. Stepping in the middle of the street, I put up my hands and I shout, "Hey, wait a minute, Sonny." He stops. He can't talk because of all the dope in his mouth in the deflated balloons.

"What you got?" I ask.

He says something, all distorted because of his mouthful, but finally I understand he's saying he's got six-dollar bags. I reach in my pocket, fumbling, making believe I'm trying to find my money. I'm playing for time, hoping the team will come back. How the hell could they miss the bastard when he's got colored balloons floating over his head?

It works. While he's waiting for me to come up with the cash, my team races up, wheels squealing. The doors of their car fly open and Anthony and Lamb dive out. Anthony immediately goes for Sonny's throat to stop him swallowing the dope in his mouth. Lamb is trying to catch the balloons which Sonny releases as soon as he sees them coming for him.

Joe Anthony and Sonny go down on the ground, struggling. Anthony's hands are around the balloon man's throat and he's choking, going blue in the face. "Spit it out, junkie bastard," Anthony is shouting. "I'll break your fucking ass."

Lamb is chasing the balloons, but they're floating higher and higher, out of his reach.

Suddenly, Sonny relaxes and gurgles out three small balloons which Joe Anthony snatches up. They cuff the balloon man and toss him in the car, but now they've got a problem. They can't get the bike into the car. There's only one way to get the English racer to the stationhouse.

Joe Anthony, in his hundred-dollar suit, his silk shirt and tie, his patent leather shoes and his cashmere topcoat, he

159

climbs onto the bike and starts riding it behind the car to the precinct. He's some sight. He isn't too good at riding a bike, but he makes it.

At the stationhouse, they question Sonny and he tells them he makes more than $200 a day selling his colored balloons. Seven days a week, he works, at $200 a day.

10

I go to work with a gun. Maybe other people go to work with a briefcase or an umbrella. I go to work with a gun and I know what a gun can do.

But, on the Staten Island connection, I don't wear it. The Narcotics Bureau downtown gets word that stuff is surfacing on Staten Island and they decide to send an undercover detective out to find where it's coming from. Me.

At the time, the Bronx is too hot for me, but I'm working with different back-up teams in Brooklyn, Queens and Manhattan. I'm putting in ten to twelve hours a day, real busy. Staten Island sounds good. The DA's office out there has a reputation for taking care of cops sent out from Manhattan, good meals, good accommodation, tender loving care.

I start to wind up my other cases and then I go out to the island. I make a meet with an assistant district attorney called McGovern and an inspector at the courthouse. McGovern has this elaborate room with lots of books all over the place and they treat me good. They offer me coffee and we start talking.

There's a third guy there, a youngster, and I dig him to be a junkie. He's an informer who's trying to get a lighter sentence by giving us information about the junk scene on the island.

McGovern's a nice guy with no bullshit. He treats me like a right guy even though I'm unshaven and dressed in old clothes so that I look more like a junkie than their informer. The junkie says you can buy stuff around Mariners Harbor on the north shore and he gives us a name, Frank Conte.

"Listen," I say, "I can't commute out here all the time. How about me taking a room here?" They agree and they get me a room in a swank motel, with TV and wall-to-wall carpeting and you only have to lift the phone to get meals in your room. After Harlem and Bedford-Stuyvesant and the South Bronx, this is really living!

I go back to the Narcotics Bureau to clear up some paperwork and report on the Staten Island situation. A sergeant calls me in. He's a Nazi but he likes me. He's always trying to prove he's a real tough guy, a guy from the streets, although the only fighting he does is with pencils and a typewriter in the back office.

He's always grabbing my hand to prove he's stronger but, fuck him, I always beat him. I don't give a fuck if he's a sergeant.

He says to me, "Hey, Tony, that Staten Island thing . . . you're gonna have Rick Pepe working with you."

I turn round and I say, "What? What's that you say? I don't need no help." Am I pissed off! I don't want to work with this fucking Rick Pepe. He's not a bad cop, he's aggressive himself. But it's his attitude. He's very loud. He comes in the office . . . he's screaming all the time, he's always jitterbugging up and down the aisle. He never takes anything serious. He doesn't use his brains.

I tell the sergeant there's no need for another man. I work best alone. I tell him it's a bullshit case, no problem. I tell him all I have to do is go around the bars, find out who's selling, buy from him and wrap it up. It shouldn't take more than a couple of weeks. I tell him I didn't have another undercover guy with me when I was making buys in Manhattan, Queens and Brooklyn. Why do I need a guy now for a bullshit case on Staten Island?

I know what it is. This guy, Rick Pepe, wants to have a good time out on Staten Island, staying at the motel, touring the bars. The end of it is, I'm forced to have Pepe with me. I just don't like the guy. If I'm working alone and I make a mistake, well, I'm the guy who's going to suffer. I don't want to suffer from some other bastard's mistake.

This Mariners Harbor is no vacation resort, whatever it sounds like. It's all broken-down waterfront, rundown homes, disused drydocks, rusting hulks, just over the Bayonne Bridge from New Jersey. That's where a lot of the guys who drink around Mariners Harbor come from, New Jersey.

And the bars . . . the bars are real buckets of blood. Specially on Friday nights. Their idea of a perfect Friday night is a big fistfight, with plenty of blood and some broken bones to top it all off. The guys wear shirts with the sleeves taken off so they can show off their tattoos. Most people, when they think of Staten Island, they think of open spaces and big houses with lots of grass all around. That's not Mariners Harbor.

We decide to be hoods from New Jersey, looking to cop some stuff. We dress real sharp. Like the Mafiosa. We're both dark.

Then we start buying drinks around the bars, making contacts, checking over the scene. There's narcotics around, no doubt about it. But I'm getting pissed off with Pepe. He sashays around, talking to the girls, making a lot of noise,

163

breaking the number one rule for an undercover agent—
never make yourself conspicuous until you know the scene.
He makes stupid statements. First, he says we're from New
York and then he says we're from New Jersey. He can't get
his goddam story straight. He doesn't care.

There's real static between us throughout the case. But I'll
say this, even Pepe would've given his life for me. I think
so, anyway. And I'd give my life for him, and that's the story
of all cops. Whether you like each other, whether you're
white or black, something happens to you when you become
a cop. If the two of you are cops, that's it. The allegiance is
greater than to your wife. Hell, sometimes your life depends
on it.

Pepe is worrying me, though. He's too hot on the girls in
the bars. Let me tell you about these girls. Their idea of a fun
time is to get two guys fighting over them. That sort of thing
we don't need. I tell him to lay off.

"Shit, man," he says, "what're you talking about? We're
gonna have a ball." We sure did.

We're in the Holland Bar on Holland Avenue, a real dive,
and we drift into the back room where there's a juke box and
dancing. Pepe's feeling good. "Look at these girls," he says,
practically panting.

This girl, about nineteen, gets up and starts dancing to the
juke box. It's playing "Night Train," with all that sexy boom,
boom. She's wearing a silk blouse, two sizes small on her. She
has a pair of headlights! She's got a black leather skirt and
she starts gyrating, grinding away and staring at us. She's
trying to provoke us and she's succeeding. Pepe goes out of
his bird. I don't know which to watch, her grinding or Pepe's
face. His eyes are popping. I know he's going to do something stupid.

I say to Pepe, "Cool it, man. The guys are gonna take

you." He doesn't listen. He moves until he's real close to her. I know she's got to have a boy friend in the crowd of guys and I know they're looking for any excuse for a fight. Now, she's wiggling and dancing all around him. He's smiling stupidly at her.

The guys are gathering, all whispering together. I know they're going to grab us and beat the hell out of us. Pepe doesn't know or he doesn't care. Now he's a sex maniac . . . He's in heat.

I go over to him and I say, "I'm getting out of here through that side door. Follow me in thirty seconds." The silly bastard just shrugs. Some of the guys are moving slowly towards the side door to cut us off, but I beat them to it.

I go out and I run to the car and I start it up. I hear noises, screams and bottles smashing and then here comes Pepe running, holding his face. He's got a big welt on his cheek. He jumps in the car and I start to accelerate away. Thank God, the motor works. Following Pepe out of the side door, come half a dozen of these punks, in their sleeveless shirts, waving broken bottles. They can't catch us and we get away fast. I'm mad. Now we can't go back there for a couple of days until it's cooled off, and it's the most likely place around to cop some stuff.

I tell this to Pepe and that doesn't improve the static between us either. A few days later, we go back to the same bar. The punks aren't there. We start to spread some money around, buying drinks, talking, making pals. Things go well. We ask where we can cop some stuff.

We've been in a lot of bars around there, spreading bread, saying we're looking for junk. Now we get a bite.

A young guy comes up to us and says, "Hey, man, I hear you're looking for stuff." I look at him and I say, "What're you drinking?" He's drinking beer but now, seeing we're buying, he switches to Scotch on the rocks.

He says his name is Frankie Conte. Click! I remember the informer in McGovern's office tipped the name Frank Conte and here's the guy. "What've you got?" I ask.

He says, "Anything you want." I say, "I'm looking for pure."

He says, "How much you want?" I say, "A key."

Wow, that does it. A kilo! His eyes open up wide. I get the idea he never had a big proposition like this before. He says he can get it. He has another Scotch on us. He says his connection will see us in a couple of days. A couple of meets are set up, but the connection never shows.

Then Conte tells us to be in our car outside the Port Richmond Clipper Diner on Richmond Terrace at 11 P.M.

We're there on time. There's a bunch of punks looking like Hells Angels hanging around the entrance. Out from the diner comes Frank Conte. "Hello, Frankie," I say. "Where's your connection?"

"He's not here yet," he says, "we gotta wait a while." He tells us to pull up a little way from the diner. We don't say much, waiting. He says his connection's name is Lenny, then he goes back to the punks.

Pepe starts to say he's hungry, he wants to get a hamburger. Oh, man. I promise him steak later, but he goes on complaining that he wants to eat now. Of all times to go and get a fucking hamburger. We're waiting for a dope pusher to come in from Manhattan. He's going to sell us a kilo of stuff. We've got two dozen killers hanging around outside the diner. And Pepe wants to get out and get a hamburger. That really pisses me off. I tell him so, and he stays where he is. I swear to myself I'll never work with another undercover man again.

A car pulls in back of us. Frankie goes over to it and then brings over this guy. He looks like a racketeer out of Hollywood. He's wearing a fedora, pin-striped silk suit, white on white shirt and pointy patent leather shoes. A very thin guy, with a sharp nose. He looks like very bad news.

Frankie introduces him as Lenny and I introduce myself as Tony Solo and give Pepe some bullshit name. They both get in our car, Frankie behind me and Lenny behind Pepe, who's at the wheel. It's a four-door Ford. Lenny does all the talking. He asks where we're from. New Jersey, I say. But where? All over, I say. I'd told Pepe to leave the talking to me.

Lenny wants to know what we're doing on the Island. I say, the same as him, dealing. I say New York's too hot. Now Pepe butts in. He says we use stuff ourselves, which is a stupid thing to say. If they want us to shoot up with them, how the hell do we get out of it?

I say, "We only chip junk, no mainlining." To myself, I'm cursing this ignorant Pepe. Lenny wants to know if we've got the money. He wants to see it. "We don't go nowhere if you don't show your money," he says. "I don't know if you're bullshitting me or not."

I take $300 from my money belt, mostly $1 bills with some tens. It's dark in the car and he sees enough to be impressed. "Okay, I believe you," he says, "you gotta understand, Solo, maybe I get you the junk and then maybe you might take me off for the junk. Okay, drive off." Pepe drives off.

Lenny starts throwing names at us, asking us if we know them. I keep saying I don't know any of them. But Pepe can't keep his yap shut. Lenny asks if we know Dean Belli. Pepe says, "Sure."

Lenny's voice goes very quiet and he says, "Where d'you know Dean Belli from?"

Pepe says, "I know him from the Island." I'm looking at this nut, Pepe. "We don't know any Dean Belli," I say.

He says, "Yeah, you know, that fat Italian guy."

Lenny says, "What d'you mean? Dean Belli's a colored guy. He's doing time. Some undercover cops busted him." I almost shit a brick. I change the subject, wanting to know if the stuff is real pure. I'm hoping he'll forget what Pepe said. But Lenny goes on asking questions. "Have you been on Staten Island before?" he asks.

Now Pepe really blows it. He chirps up, "Sure, man, I used to have a beat out here." Now there's a real nasty silence. When Pepe used the word "beat," he could have just been using an expression. But he could also have been referring to a police beat. Oh, man! Never again. I can feel the suspicion growing like a weed.

"Look," I cut in, "you been asking a lot of questions. We showed you the money, let's go."

"By the way," Lenny says, "have you guys got any guns on you?" I say, "No, we don't have no guns." We aren't carrying any. But we do have guns under the front seat, covered by a rag.

Lenny says, "Okay, but before we take the ferry, I wanna take a shot. I'm getting sick 'cause I use stuff." By now, we're driving back by the diner. He directs Pepe to drive around the corner and pull up off the road in this secluded spot under a railroad trestle. It's dark, no light at all. Lenny tells Frankie, "Go out and get the stuff."

Frankie comes back from the darkness and in his hand he's got a package. I know something's wrong. It's too quiet now. Lenny says, "We're gonna cook up some junk now and we're gonna shoot up."

I hear a click, a metallic click, and the next thing is I feel a cold hard object at the base of my neck. It's Conte, behind me. "Give me the money belt. Hurry up," he says. I'm frozen stiff. "The guy's got a gun," I say to Pepe. "Don't move."

Then I say, "Listen, you guys, we're cops. We're detectives. Put away the gun." Pepe is screaming, "Listen, listen, we're cops!"

The next thing, Lenny shouts, "Frankie, burn 'em! Burn 'em, Frankie!"

While he's still shouting, I twist around and throw my left hand back for the gun. I grab the gun, a silver .38 revolver. Through the grace of God, my thumb slides down to the base of the hammer. He pulls the trigger and the hammer goes forward. But instead of hitting the bullet, the pin mashes into my thumb up to the bone. Blood spatters all over the place.

Still holding the gun, I turn right around and start beating the piss out of him. I knock him cold, finally, with his own gun. The door on his side breaks open and he topples out to the ground.

Pepe is fighting with Lenny, who is halfway out of the window on his side. Lenny pulls his foot back and kicks Pepe in the jaw. I go over the top of the car and I smash Lenny in the face. He goes down and I follow him, giving him a kick to make sure.

I look around and see Frankie is up and running. I throw a shot after him from his own gun. The bullet ricochets off a fence with a whining sound, real loud. Frankie stops and he throws up his hands. "Don't shoot, don't shoot," he shouts. "You've got me." I run up to him and I give him a kick. He doubles up.

I drag him back to the car where Pepe's holding Lenny. Lights are going on in nearby houses and a few minutes later uniformed cops show up in patrol cars. They've got drawn guns. This sort of thing doesn't happen on Staten Island. They're more used to barking dog complaints. We have to prove to them that we're cops because we look more like hoods in our gangster disguises than the real bad guys.

We just stand there with our prisoners while they surround us, pointing their guns at us. They're hiding behind their cars as if we're the Dalton Gang. "Throw your guns out," some cop yells, and we do. We can't show them our badges because we've got them in the trunk of the car. They open the trunk, find the badges and start to believe we might be the good guys.

My hand's still bleeding, so I'm taken to a hospital where five stitches are inserted. The mark's still there today.

At the 120th Precinct, an old detective, a guy with a cigar and a big pot belly, he says, "What happened, kid?" I tell him Frankie tried to kill us.

"He's a cop fighter?"

I say, "He wanted to be a cop killer."

This detective stares at me. "You mean to tell me, you let him come in alive?" he demands. "A guy who tried to burn you?"

He says, "Come with me, kid, and bring that little punk with you." I bring Frankie with me and we follow him out of a side door and the next thing you know we're getting into this detective's car. He drives us to a beach, a very lonely place.

We get out. Frankie doesn't know what's going on. Neither do I. He thinks maybe he's going to get a beating. This detective takes the revolver that Frankie tried to use on me and he hands it to me. "Okay, kid," he says, "do it." This detective wants me to blow away Frankie.

I can't believe it. I say, "Wait a minute, pal, I can't do that. I'm not squeamish . . . don't get me wrong. I don't mind if it's in the heat of a fight or something to protect myself . . . I'm capable of doing something like this. But not murder."

The detective says, "Listen, kid, you're not committing no murder. This guy's a killer. I know about him. He mugs people. He stabs old ladies in the street."

He turns on Frankie and he says, "Okay, Frankie, run, Frankie, run, damn you." Conte goes crazy. "Don't do it," he pleads. "Don't do it."

"Frankie," shouts the detective, "run. Run now!"

Frankie won't run and the detective says again, "Do it, kid, burn him." I say, "I can't do it, pal."

He grabs the gun from me and says, "Okay, I'll do it." I see he's raising it at Frankie and I go for him. We struggle for the gun for a moment, then we calm down and I tell Frankie to get in the car. We all get back in and the detective turns round and says to Frankie, "You're lucky; you're very lucky, you punk." Then he throws a right hook to Frankie's chest, knocking the wind out of him.

I never found out whether this detective was serious when he told me to burn Frankie, or whether he just wanted to put the fear of God into him. I reported it anyway. Later, at the stationhouse, reporters show up and there's the assistant DA, McGovern, and the inspector. Frankie and Lenny are booked on charges of attempted murder and a half dozen other charges. In front of everybody, Pepe comes over to me and you know what he says? He says, "Solo and me, we don't get along. But you know, I love him 'cause he saved my life."

Then, I swear to God, he kisses me full on the mouth. Right on the fucking mouth, in front of the reporters, McGovern and the inspector. Ech! Isn't that enough to make me want to work alone?

11

THERE'S a lot of good guys in the narcotics division and Patsy Mazza is one of them. I break him in for undercover work and we work together on the street, but this particular time we're assigned to the Special Investigating Unit.

Patsy is Italian-American like me, but I think he's more Italian than American. He's the funniest sonofabitch I've ever met, always with a joke even though he's doing the same kind of dangerous work I'm doing.

While we're with the SIU, we work on a case involving a large shipment of hashish which is coming into New York from South America. We learn it'll be coming in on a cargo ship called the *Bagota* which is to dock in Brooklyn on Pier 4. We put a lot of work into this case and when the ship is due to dock, we're there waiting.

Among the things we've found out is that the hash will be brought ashore by a seaman and thrown over a fence to avoid the customs. We know exactly the spot where the stuff will come flying over.

The ship shows up in the river but it doesn't come in to dock. There's a longshoreman's strike so she just stands out there waiting.

The strike is supposed to be settled soon and then she'll come in, but in the meantime she stays anchored in the river and we wait around the pier. By 1 A.M. there's still no settlement and Patsy and I are exhausted because we've been missing a lot of sleep on this case.

"Frig this," Patsy says. "Let's get outta here. We'll leave the stool pigeon here and go home. They probably aren't gonna settle this goddam strike until tomorrow now. If anything happens, the stool can call us back."

He's right. If we don't catch up on some sleep, we'll be too tired to put the cuffs on anybody. Off we go. I get home and find a note left by Helen, who's asleep. She tells me there's some chicken in the oven waiting to be warmed up for a meal. I undress, put on my pajamas and settle down in front of the late, late show with my chicken and a cup of coffee.

I'm just finishing the meal at around 3 A.M. when Patsy rings me. "Tony," he says urgently, "the boat's moving. It's coming in to dock. The informer just called me. They must have settled the strike. You'd better get down there."

"I'm on my way, Patsy," I say. I leave the TV on, the dishes in the living room, and in five minutes I'm dressed and on my way.

In the car with me is my sawed-off shotgun in its case. It's not loaded, but I have some of those Number 4 Magnum shells with me, with the twenty-eight ball bearings in each shell.

I push my little car real fast, and when I hit the Harlem River Drive I'm doing 70 m.p.h. easy. This is going to be a good arrest and I want to be in on it. While I'm driving, I keep my eye on the rear-view mirror because I don't want a hassle with any traffic cops. If they pull me over, that's wasted time while I explain who I am and why I'm speeding.

173

On the East River Drive, I see a pair of headlights behind me and I say to myself, oh, shit, it's the cops. The car's coming fast and it's got to be the cops. Passing East 79th Street, the car behind's still coming and now I'm sure they're clocking me. My foot eases off the accelerator and my car slows down to 60, 50, 40 m.p.h. The car is right behind me now but it doesn't try to come alongside and order me over to the side. It has its brights on and the lights in my mirror are blinding me.

I really slow down, to 30 and then 20 m.p.h. What the hell is going on? I think. The car behind is tailgating me.

Suddenly, I get jolted. The driver behind accelerates and smashes into my rear bumper. He drops back and he does it again, ramming into my rear. He comes so hard my trunk snaps open so I can't see through my mirror. All I've got now is the side-view mirror.

These can't be cops, not unless there's a couple of patrolmen escaped from Bellevue's psycho ward. I start to speed up with my trunk door bouncing up and down and they come after me. I'm not going to stop on the East River Drive at 4 A.M., no, sir. On top of that, I've got to get to that pier as fast as possible. It's a big case for me.

After that ramming, I'm scared. I don't know what the hell is going on. As I speed up, I reach back and bring the case containing my shotgun from the back seat and put it alongside me. I start to unbuckle the straps, but I don't take the gun out. I think I can get away from the guys. I can't.

As we approach the downtown area, the car behind swings out and comes abreast of me. There's a bunch of guys inside and those on the passenger side are hanging out of the windows flagging me down. "Pull over, pull over!" they're shouting. It's a blue kidney-cutter Buick.

I try to accelerate away from them, but my old car doesn't

have the power the Buick has. They're still abreast of me and then they come at me, hitting my left fender, trying to force me over. I keep going and they come at me again. Another crash of metal as they hit. My car's beginning to look as though it's ready for the junk yard. All the left side is crumpled and there's my trunk door flying about in the breeze.

Near Houston Street, they ram me again and I'm forced over against the guard wall until I'm scraping it. I stop. The Buick pulls alongside and the four doors open. Six guys pile out and one of them comes over to me. "Hey, man," he says, "what's the matter with you? You crazy? You hit my car back there. Get out and show me your license."

I know what it's all about now. These guys are highwaymen. These bastards hang around the parkways and wait for a lone car, best of all a woman driver. They force it over and rob the driver. No cops around at that time in the morning. Nobody.

I won't get out of the car. Behind me, I can hear one of the guys fumbling around in my trunk. "Listen, you bastards," I say. "I'm a police officer and I'm headed for an emergency." I show my badge, but these guys don't care . . . they want trouble. "You a cop?" one of them says. "If you a cop, you shoot me right here!" And he points a finger at his forehead. Another of them pulls one of my windshield wipers out and he breaks it. Then he reaches out and snaps off my radio aerial. I'm really pissed off now, but I still don't want to pull a gun on them. If I do that, I know I'm going to have to shoot at least one of them . . . there's too many for me to handle and they don't care if I do have a gun. Better for me to try and get away from them. Maybe I didn't handle it the best way, but I was thinking all the time of getting to Brooklyn.

One of the guys is trying to open the door on my right side.

175

Suddenly, I put the car in gear and I take off again. The Houston Street exit is just ahead and I go off the East River Drive, down the ramp and through a red light. I'm hoping I've lost the bastards. There's no sign of them in my side mirror, so I swing back onto the East River Drive at the next entry. All of a sudden, they're right behind me. They must have stayed up on the drive and seen what I did.

But now I have a chance. As fast as I can, I turn off the drive and take the exit for the Brooklyn Bridge. If I can get over to Brooklyn, Patsy Mazza will help me take care of these sonsofbitches. It's no good. They're right on top of me. I pull out the shotgun from its case and break it open. Fumbling in my pockets while I'm driving, I take two shells from my pockets and load the gun, snapping it closed. By now, I'm up on the bridge itself and they're coming up alongside me again.

My hands are sweating. I'm as scared as I've ever been. I've got my left hand on the steering wheel, my right hand holding the gun which I bring over until it's poking out the window, resting on the door. I'm doing about 45 m.p.h. and they're overtaking me, coming alongside. They're hanging out of the car windows, one of them holding a jack handle, all screaming in Spanish.

My finger's on the trigger. Already, I'm imagining the noise when I let loose with both barrels.

Bang! But the noise doesn't come from my gun. I haven't pulled the trigger. It comes from their car, and at first I think they're shooting at me. Their car is no longer abreast . . . it suddenly drops back. In my side mirror, I see what's happened. Their front nearside tire has blown . . . the tire on the side where they were ramming me . . . I can see the black rubber flapping.

While I'm still staring into the mirror, their car careens to the side of the bridge, skids around and then turns right over onto its back. There's a jangling of metal and I can see a cloud of dust coming up from the wrecked car. I stop and stick my head out through the side window. The punks come tumbling out of the wreck. None of the bastards can be hurt bad because they all start running back to the Manhattan side.

The other side of the bridge, I call in an alarm on the accident, tell the cops who I am and race off to Brooklyn and the dock. When Patsy Mazza sees my car, all falling apart, he says, "What the hell happened to you?" I tell him, and Patsy he just laughs. "Schiano," he says, "you're full of shit. Stop with that bull." He won't believe me.

It's a helluva way to get to a job, but we make the arrest and grab the hash, a suitcase full.

It comes sailing over the fence in a duffle bag while we're watching from inside a parked panel truck. We let it lie there and just wait in our truck, which has a radio and a one-way window where you can look out but you can't look in. Hours later, up comes a car and a guy gets out to pick up the duffle bag. We grab him and the hash with no trouble.

When it's all over, I head back for Manhattan. On the bridge, I see the Buick's still there, on its back with traffic cones around it and a couple of uniformed cops on the scene. I pull over to the side and go take a look. There's no license plates, so there's no way of telling who it belongs to. Inside, I see a spatter of blood. One of the bastards was hurt—at least one of them.

The cops on the scene tell me there's nobody there when they roll up. We check all the hospitals, but there's nobody like these punks come in. I guess they're scared to get treatment because of the questions they'd get hit with.

All that so I can grab a suitcase of hash? Where's the harm

in some hash? Why don't they change the laws and make grass legal? Bullshit. It may be different on a campus or on the upper East Side. But every junkie I ever met, he started on grass. It's pretty good for helping you forget your problems. Hash, that's even better. Okay, so why not chip a bit of heroin . . . put some on the point of a needle and scratch it into the skin up by the shoulder. The high comes slow that way, nice and slow. But then you want some more, so why not inject it into the veins? Zap! It's got you. I've been involved in the arrest of hundreds of pushers, nearly all of them junkies themselves, and every one I've talked to, he started on grass.

In some ways, there's more excuse for a junkie pusher. He often does it to support his own habit. What's the excuse for a guy who makes money selling grass? He just wants the easy buck. And if his customer switches to the big H, well, that's too bad.

Informers . . . I've worked with a lot of them and I've talked to them as we operated on the street, contacting pushers, making buys. There was Johnny, a blond-haired youngster who agreed to work off his case by going on the street with me and my team. I don't know why, but he really worked. He was always at the meet early. He went all the way.

Even when he was sick, doubled up with cramps, he'd keep working. He'd be crying, but he'd still work. I asked him once why he was so gung-ho and he mumbled something about we were the first cops who had treated him like a human being. Maybe that was it, maybe it was something else.

Anyway, we became good friends, Johnny and me. When we had a pusher ready to be picked up, I'd stay and keep an

178

eye on him while Johnny went back to tell the back-up team. He used to hide my two-way radio in his waistband under his shirt so we could stay in touch with the team.

Johnny came from a broken home. He had an alcoholic father who constantly beat up his mother. Eventually, the father took off, leaving Johnny alone with his mother. They were very close. He took me home once and I met her. Always, when he had some money, he'd send some to her, maybe $5 or $10.

I trusted Johnny, and that's saying something for a junkie informer. This one time, we go to a rooming house to make a buy and as we're coming back down the stairs, we find the way blocked by three guys. They're after the dope and the money they think we have. We look back and there are two guys above us.

Johnny takes out the two-way radio and they want that, too. He tells them it's a transistor radio and then he goes into action.

He smashes one of the guys below us with the radio, right in the puss, and he jumps at the other two, knocking them over.

"Run, Tony," he shouts. He got his arms around the necks of two of them. "Go on, Tony," he yells. I hesitate and he yells again. I dash out, get the team and we go rushing back. We find Johnny. His face is messed up, all bloody, and we discover later his nose is broken. Two of his teeth are broken, but he smiles as we carry him out of the building and take him to a hospital. He's still got my two-way radio . . . he doesn't give that up.

Always, when we've finished our buys for the day, the team and me, we chip in with some money for Johnny. We tell him to use it to pay his rent or buy some clothes or get them cleaned or have a good meal. He says he will, but I know he's going to go and buy some stuff. He's got a monkey on his back that's more like a gorilla. He's got a fantastic habit. He cooks up with ten to fifteen decks and shoots up the lot. His whole body is covered with sores where he's injected himself.

Sometimes, he cries and he says to me, "Tony, I know I'm gone now. I'm a living dead man. But, you know, the thing I'm really scared of is that I'll hurt somebody, getting my money." That's why he gets his buy-money from burglaries, not from robberies. He says he can make more that way, anyway.

We're sitting on a stoop one time and I ask him how it feels that first time he gets a high from heroin. A lot of junkies have told me different things but this Johnny, he puts it this way: "It's like having a tearing toothache and suddenly it goes. It's like having a fractured leg and suddenly it's back together again.

"You're calm and there are no problems. Everything's sweet and beautiful.

"But when you're sick, forget it. It's like every square inch of your body hurts. It's like you've been run over by a truck. You want to throw up, but there's nothing to throw up. Man, compared with that, death is nothing. There's no medicine for this sickness but more junk."

Johnny, after he's worked with us, he seems to decide he likes cops. Once, when he's coming to make a meet with us, he sees a patrolman having trouble with three young punks. One of the punks pushes the cop so that he falls and then they all jump on him, punching him around the face. Johnny goes to a telephone and he puts in a call, "Assist patrolman." Within minutes half a dozen patrol cars scream up, so quick that the punks are still there and the cops grab them.

Another time, after we work nearly fifteen hours at a stretch, I say to Johnny, "Come on, kid, let's go and have a nice big meal. I feel in the mood for it."

"Nah," he says, "thanks, Tony, but I don't really want to. Save your money." I won't let it alone.

"Come on," I say, "I want you to have dinner with me." Still he shrugs it off but eventually, when I keep on at him, he agrees to come. We go to a posh midtown restaurant. Of course, we don't look too hot, in our greasy old clothes. The waiters don't want to serve us. To be honest, we both smell a bit. They stick us in a corner behind a large plant so that their other customers won't have to look at us. We know what it's all about but, fuck them, we don't care.

The waiter keeps us hanging around, but then he comes and takes our order. We have cocktails, the whole bit.

We both have steak and potatoes, followed by strawberry cake with ice cream, followed by coffee, topped off by another drink. I buy Johnny a pack of cigarettes and he lights up and sits back in his chair and he really seems to be enjoying himself. We talk about our lives and then the bill comes and I'm paying it when Johnny gets up and says, "Hey, Tony, excuse me a moment . . . I'll be right back."

I think he's going to take a leak, but I see him heading for the door of the restaurant. The waiter brings me my change and I leave a tip, not too much . . . and go after Johnny. At the front of the restaurant there is a big window and I look through it. Johnny's at the curb, throwing up all that expensive dinner into the gutter.

He's very apologetic when he sees me. "I'm sorry, Tony," he says. "I only came and ate with you because you made such a big deal out of it. I really am sorry, but I couldn't hold it down."

181

"That's okay, Johnny," I say. "Let's go." And Johnny, he goes off. I guess he goes to find his connection.

Later, Johnny is arrested and he goes to jail. We write to each other and occasionally I send him a bit of money. When he comes out, he wants to straighten out and he joins one of these drug programs. The last I hear of him, he's doing well. But, it's mostly bullshit about junkies being able to kick the habit. Once you're hooked, that's it.

Another informer. A kid called Hackey. We're waiting on McDougal Street in the Village for a connection. He starts fidgeting. "What's the matter, Hackey?" I ask. He's a junkie, but he's supposed to be going straight.

"Nothing," he says. But I can tell he's edgy.

A few moments later, he says, "Listen, Tony, I gotta go take a piss. Where can I go?"

I shrug. I'm looking for the connection.

"Listen," he says. "I'm going across to that hallway. I can take a leak in there."

"Okay," I say. "But don't be long. I need you here when the connection shows up."

He goes across the street and up the steps into the hallway. I wait and time goes by and still Hackey doesn't come back. I start to wonder if he's taken off on me. I go over and walk up the steps and I go into the hallway.

At the end of the hallway, I see Hackey. He's cooking up. He's got a tourniquet around his bare arm. He's using his belt, with one end gripped between his teeth.

The guy's supposed to be clean and here he is shooting up. I'm real pissed off.

"You sonofabitch," I shout. I grab him and I throw him against the wall and I kick away the syringe, the needle, the cooking cap and the match he's got burning. "What's the

182

matter?" I yell. "Are you crazy or something? I thought you were gonna make it.

"Here I'm trying to help you, and other cops have tried to help you, and all the time you're back on the stuff."

He lunges at me and he grabs me by my jacket and he starts shaking me and the tears are pouring from his eyes.

"Don't you understand?" he screams. "I'm a dead man. I'm dead. Don't you understand? Get the fuck out of here. Nobody wants me—no father, mother, no wife, child. I'm a dead man."

He pushes me away, so that I stagger back and he gets down on his hands and knees and tries to pick up his equipment. He's putting the needle and the syringe back together. And all the time he's weeping and saying, "Let me alone. Get the fuck out of here."

There's nothing I can do. I look down at him and then walk out.

I have to laugh when I hear these social workers and psychoanalysts and whatnot on TV and radio or read what they have to say in the papers. They say a junkie can quit. Bullshit. For a time, maybe. When a guy's been on heroin for a while, he just can't quit . . . not for good. Something happens to the body of an addict. He becomes a different animal altogether. When a guy goes on the stuff, that's it.

Okay, maybe there's one chance if he gives it up and goes to another environment, far away from the place where he used to shoot up. But 99 percent of junkies can't do that. They end up back on the street.

I knew an old-timer called Billy. He told me he had been on the stuff since he was nine years old . . . he was turned on to opium by some woman. He stayed on opium until he was fourteen and then he went into heroin. Later, he got fourteen years in Dannemora prison upstate. In that time, he told me, he never once used the stuff, but the first thing he did when he got out, he went immediately to a cooker and he shot up. He got his first fix in some cellar while he still had his prison suitcase with him.

Knowing that, knowing how many guys have gone from grass to heroin, I take marijuana cases as seriously as I take heroin cases. I've found that the guys who push grass are sometimes even more vicious than junkie pushers.

Like the time I'm working with Jack Nelson, the guy who wins the Medal of Honor, and his partner, Vinnie Belanti, up in the Bronx. They get hold of a faggot hairdresser who agrees to work off his arrest by giving up his connections. I'm brought in to work undercover with this hairdresser and this time I can look pretty good, with trimmed hair, a good shave and sporty clothes. This fag . . . his name is Alice . . . he's real nervous about the whole thing when I first meet him outside the salon where he works.

He won't talk on the street and he takes me to his apartment while Jack Nelson and Belanti wait outside. Alice is something. His place is decorated exclusively in pink, with knickknacks a woman would have. He primps his hair a bit in front of a mirror and then he says, "Please have a seat . . . I want to make myself comfortable." He lisps like Princess.

He takes off his silk shirt and his pants, and underneath he's wearing a pair of women's panties and long stockings attached to that girdle thing that looks like an octopus. I say to myself, this guy is really sick. I get a little worried. But he leaves his underclothes on and drapes himself in a robe. "Can I offer you a drink?" he wants to know. Bullshit, I say to myself, I'm not drinking with this guy up here. I refuse.

He's nervous as hell. "I need one," he says, and he goes to a cabinet and pours himself half a glass of Scotch, which he knocks off in one gulp. He's in a bad way.

"What's the matter, Alice?" I say.

"I never did this before," he says. "You know those guys I deal with, they're bad guys." He's pacing up and down the pink room. I make him sit down and try to relax him. Then I ask him what he's got.

He takes a deep breath and he says, "I know two fellows who're selling large amounts of grass. They're the guys I bought from before I got arrested."

"Names?"

He hesitates, then he says, "Byron Lint and a fellow called Barry. They work together."

"When can I meet them?"

"They're coming here to my apartment tonight," he says.

"Great. Do they know about me? That I want to buy?"

"Yeah," he says. "I told them I've got a guy who wants to buy a lot. I told them you'd be here tonight."

Good. I tell him I'll be back later and that night I'm back sitting in his pink apartment when there's a knock on the door and in come two guys. I'm surprised. I expect two hard guys, but these aren't. They're young, well-dressed and immediately I figure they're fags like Alice. This Byron, he's about twenty-two and he's got bright blond hair, combed flat. Barry is about the same age, but he's dark. Both hairstylists.

I find out later they both come from wealthy families. Alice introduces us and he tells these two I'm Tony Solo, that I'm down from the Catskills where I supply grass to the big hotels and that I need a new connection because my old one has been arrested. I tell them, yeah I want to buy.

185

"How much d'you want?" Byron says.

"I can handle 100 pounds or more," I say. I'm trying to impress them. When I say that, this guy Byron, his eyes pop open, and Barry's staring at me, too.

"You got that kind of money?" Barry wants to know.

"Sure I have," I say. "I'm ready right now." I reach into my pocket and take out a roll of bills and flash it at them. I'm taking a chance doing this, I know, but I feel I've got things under control. Alice knows I'm a cop and he's not going to let these two try to take me off in his apartment.

"How much can you get me?" I say.

"As much as you want," Byron says, "and it's real good stuff."

"How much d'you charge?"

"A half ounce is $25," he says.

"What! I can get that for $20," I say. "Forget it."

"Yeah, but this is the real thing. Panamanian Red."

Barry comes on strong. "If he don't want it, let's forget it."

"I'll tell you what," I say, "let me buy a taste."

Byron takes out a plastic bag and he says, "Okay, you can have a taste of this. This is $8 . . . you can get about twenty-five smokes out of this."

I buy it and tell them I'll try it on my customers up north. If there's no static, I'll be back for more in a couple of days. I tell them I'll see them in Alice's apartment at 6 P.M. two days later. That's settled and they leave.

They're happy, but Alice is not. "You're not meeting here," he says after he's closed the door on them. "I don't want no more to do with it. They'll kill me, I know it. They may not look much, but they're killers." He's crying. I try to calm him, but it don't work. Finally, I have to get tough and chastise him. When I leave, he's agreed to the meet.

Two days later, Byron turns up at the apartment. He sure smells nice. I guess it's the perfume and stuff they have in hairdressing salons. More negotiations come in the next few days, including cloak-and-dagger meetings on street corners. Crazy. I buy small amounts, but I'm not getting to his connection, and that's what it's all about. This one time, on a street corner, Jerome Avenue and Fordham Road, I buy $25 worth and then I say, "Hey, man, what about the connection . . . when am I gonna meet him?"

"You decided how much you want?" he says.

"About two pounds," I say. "Maybe even three."

"Okay, let me call you."

"I move around." I say quickly, "I'll have to call you." It's stupid of him, but he gives me his home phone number and tells me to call him two nights later. With his number, he can never get away from us. But now we have a problem. To buy two or three pounds of grass, we need more money than the department normally issues. To cover myself, I need $1,000 . . . better still, $1,500 . . . but the department won't go for it. They say they can't get that kind of money.

There's only one way. The feds. The feds always have enough money. We don't like working with these federal narcotics people because they always try to take over a case, but there's no other way. We have a meet with the feds, explain the situation, and they finally come up with $300. It's not enough, but it's better than nothing. They sure are worried about their money . . . they take the serial numbers of all the bills they give me. Then I call Byron.

"It's all set," he says. "My connection wants to meet with you. He'll do the thing with you."

"Where?"

"Jerome and Fordham again. You got the money?"

"I got it," I tell him.

The feds, the back-up team and me, we make a meet to organize ourselves. The federal narcotics guys come with three taxicabs fitted with two-way radios and there are two unmarked cars, also with radios. I wish my department had the sort of facilities these feds have.

At 7:15 that night, I'm in position on the street corner. The taxicabs and the unmarked cars are all in view, parked inconspicuously. I wait and I wait. It's 8 P.M., and still Byron doesn't show. It's 8:45 before a small rattle-trap of a car comes along and Byron shoves his head out the window. "Come on," he says. "Get in." I do what he says and we drive off, going west on Fordham Road to the Major Deegan Expressway, heading for the George Washington Bridge. Before the bridge, he takes the ramp down to the West Side Highway and as we make the big circle, I can see the taxicabs following us.

We go south and then turn off the highway to 86th Street and Central Park West, where we park. Byron seems nervous and he doesn't talk much, except to ask, "You sure you got the money?" I tell him, don't worry. We walk to a restaurant on 88th Street. There's a lot of weirdos, fags and junkies in there and I'm getting worried. Since we parked, there's no sign of the back-up teams. I'm wondering if we lost them somewhere.

We have some coffee and then we leave. Still there's no sign of the back-up teams. I'm beginning to sweat.

We go to a building on West 88th Street. Now I know the teams have lost me. There's no cars, no taxis, nothing. All that fucking organization, radio taxis, unmarked cars and still they lose me. My only reassurance is my gun, which I've got stashed away in my groin.

Byron presses a buzzer on a door on the ground floor and it's opened by his pal Barry, who goes and sticks his head into the street to check the scene. Then he takes us into this apartment, not very impressive but okay. Then I see something. On one chair is draped a soldier's uniform and near it is a large padlocked duffle bag. There's a steel helmet on the bag and on the floor is a pair of combat boots. I get nearer and I see it's an army officer's uniform. Just then a guy walks out of the kitchen, a drink in his hand. He's wearing civilian clothes, a shirt and slacks and ankle boots.

"You a soldier?" I say.

"Yeah, I'm a lieutenant," he says. He's a medium-sized guy with reddish hair, combed Caesar-fashion.

"You're on leave?"

"Yeah, I came up here to deliver some stuff." He says he's stationed down south near the Mexican border and he brings large amounts of grass up to New York to sell.

He says it's easy for him because of his officer's rank. Nobody searches him. His ambition, he says, is to make a big killing before he gets out of the army. So he needs some big connections. That's why he's interested in me. His name is Robert.

Byron does a lot of talking for me. He impresses Robert that I have a lot of money on me and that I came down from the Catskills to buy for a group up there. Robert doesn't say much. He strikes me as a very careful cat. He keeps looking me over and the time begins to drift by.

"Listen," I say finally, "you got the stuff or haven't you?"

"Take it easy," he says. "You got the money?"

Byron says, "He's got it."

"Show it to me," Robert says.

"I'm not showing you nothing until I see the merchandise," I say. We keep arguing and we're not getting any-where. So I reach into my shirt and take the $300 out of my money belt and show it to him . . . just long enough to let him know I've got a good chunk of cash . . . then I put it back in my belt.

Robert wants me to take off my coat and relax. I say no. He wants to know who I know in the neighborhood. I tell him I don't know anybody. I'm getting impatient. I don't like the way it's going.

"Why won't you take off your coat?" he says.

"Because I may have to leave here fast," I come back.

"Okay," he says, "then let me search you. I tell you, man, I don't trust you." If he searches me, he's going to find the gun and the knife. More than that, he'll find my badge. I get up abruptly as if I'm insulted.

"You ain't searching me," I say. "What sort of bullshit is this?"

"What's the harm if I just pat you down?"

"You ain't putting your hands on me." Very quick, I walk to the door and I step out into the hallway. There's a garbage can there and as quick as I can I take my gun and badge and toss them into the can. As soon as I've done this, I hear somebody behind me. It's Byron.

"Please, Solo," he says, "don't get pissed off. Try to under-stand . . . the guy is very cautious. Just let him pat you down."

"I don't want him touching me," I say. "You can do it. Go ahead." And I open up my coat for him. Byron frisks me and makes sure I don't have a piece on me. We go back to the apartment.

"He's all right," Byron says. "I searched him and he's clean."

"You sure?"

"Yeah, Robert, he's got nothing."

Barry, he gets on the phone and calls somebody, but the conversation doesn't mean anything to me. I ask what gives and Robert says the grass is being ordered. He says he doesn't keep it with him.

"Here," he says, "I want you to taste this." He lights up a big fat joint which they start to pass around. When it comes to me, I don't suck it . . . I blow into the joint so it sparks a bit like it does when you smoke one properly. I need to keep my head clear . . . I try to keep my head below all the fumes that are beginning to fill the room. Even so, some of it hits me and I get that feeling as if the soles of my feet are soft, as if I'm walking on fur.

The phone rings and Barry answers it, then he goes and whispers to Robert. They start putting on their coats, but I notice that Robert has slipped something into his waistband from a closet before he puts on his beaver skin coat. I can't see what it is.

"Come on," Robert says, "let's get outta here."

"Where are we going?" I ask.

"You want the stuff, we're gonna pick it up."

As I stand up, Robert gets on one side of me, Barry on the other. Barry nods at Robert, who then pulls out a P. 38, a pearl-handled piece which he sticks in my ribs.

"Don't make any wrong moves," he says. "I don't trust you." I'm shitting.

"Man," I say, "what are you doing? Are you crazy?"

"Listen, we're gonna go outside and we're gonna get into a car and I wanna be sure that when we get where we're going, you don't do anything stupid. If we're followed, I'm blowing you apart."

"You got nothing to worry about," I say, wondering what happened to my teams. "You're not gonna take me off?"

"No," Robert says, "I just wanna make sure we all get a fair shake out of this. I'm no fool." He's sticking the gun real hard against my ribs.

We go out of the apartment and I notice Byron is very nervous. "Did you know this was gonna happen?" I ask him. He doesn't answer. I know what's on Robert's mind. He's going to take me off for all the money he thinks I've got. We step into the street, and dammit, it's deserted. Not a car in sight . . . not even a parked car of any sort. I can imagine what my teams are doing. They must be driving up and down, looking for me.

At the car, Robert moves his gun until it's pressing against my head and we both get into the back seat. The other two sit up front, Byron behind the wheel.

Robert has the gun in his left hand, with me sitting on his right. He puts his right arm around my neck and presses the gun against my left temple. Byron has trouble starting his car, partly because it's cold and partly because he's so nervous.

"Goddamit," Robert says, "take it easy. Cool it . . . you're flooding the carburetor." Eventually, the car starts and Byron drives off. Following Robert's orders, he goes up and down the block, then around a couple of corners, then turns, while they check to see if they're being followed. All this time, that gun muzzle is pressing against my head. Robert seems satisfied and he tells Byron to drive to an address on a side street off Central Park West.

When we get there, Barry gets out, leaving the door open, and runs inside. He comes back a few minutes later with a black briefcase. I lean forward to look at it and Robert says, "Take it easy, Solo, or I'll blow your head off." We drive off.

We're on 72nd Street, going east towards Central Park West, when we have to stop for a light. "What's gonna happen?" I ask.

"Give us the money," Robert says. The gun's still at my head.

"Wait a minute, let me see the grass," I say.

"Give us the money or I'll burn you."

I reach inside my belt and give him the $300.

He opens the briefcase and inside are three large bricks of compressed grass, covered with cellophane. He gives me one of them and closes the briefcase. As he's doing this, I make a grab for the P. 38, which is no longer at my head because he's trying to close his briefcase. I get it. I smash him across the forehead with it.

I tell Byron to pull over but, instead, Byron starts through the intersection, driving wildly. Pushing the gun over the seat, I fire two shots which smash into the instrument panel. To tell the truth, I mean to hit Byron's arm but I miss. I don't touch him but he screams. The car stops. Barry's door opens and Barry tries to get out. Byron also opens his door and starts to get out. I'm there first. Barry, I smash him across the jaw with the piece and I point the P. 38 at Byron.

"You run and you get shot," I say.

I point the P. 38 into the air and I fire two more shots. Bam! Bam! Now I wait. Barry and Byron stand outside the car. Robert is still in the back seat, nursing his face. A crowd collects. I'm standing there, waving a white handkerchief in the air.

The next thing I know we're surrounded by unmarked cars and taxicabs and my teams are piling out of them. Beautiful. They've found me. They grab the three guys and the grass.

The first thing the federal agents say to me is, "Give us the

$300, please." They couldn't give a fuck about me . . . all they're interested in is the money. We all go back to the apartment where we find more grass. I have trouble recovering my gun and badge from the trash can because somebody has put more garbage on top of them. Robert is booked on charges of illegal sale of narcotics, possession of a loaded automatic and attempted assault; the other two on drug charges.

12

I'VE got scrawny legs. That's because of all the walking I have to do when I'm undercover. It's constant walking, standing, walking again, climbing tenement stairs, walking again, hanging around, walking again. But one time I get a free ride in a taxicab.

It begins when Jack Nelson asks for me to help him with an operation in the Bronx. I don't want to, because I'm busy in Manhattan and Brooklyn, but then he says the pushers he's after are selling to kids at schools and I don't like that. I've got kids of my own. He says it's heavy between 137th Street and 147th Street on Brook Avenue and St. Anne's Avenue. The schools are the Samuel Gompers High School and P.S. 37.

I say, okay. I wind up my operations . . . anyway, I'm glad to get out of Brooklyn. The court system there stinks.

After a meet with Jack Nelson and his partner, Bob Kelly, I go out on the street and spread myself around. This detective, Kelly, is completely hairless. It's some sort of illness he had as a child. The guy shines . . . like Mr. Clean.

On the street, I make my contacts and find out who's selling in the school yards. There's a dude in particular called Black Tony. Also, I find a restaurant called the Blue Sea

Restaurant, where they not only sell but package the junk. There's an old doctor in the area who's selling prescriptions for goofballs. There's plenty of doctors in the city like him.

I buy from Pepine, from Cocoa, from Jose-Luis and from Black Tony. Cocoa and Black Tony, they sell in the schoolyards because that gives them a 360-degree view around them if the cops should try to grab them. They have a better chance of getting away.

After a few weeks, I'm in real good with all the junkies and the pushers . . . in fact, some of the junkies think I'm a pusher because I have to buy heavily. The only trouble is that I have to keep finding excuses for not shooting up with any of the junkies and I wonder how long it'll be before they notice I'm never with them when they're cooking up. I keep buying. There's enough heroin around here to turn on a regiment.

When I've doubled up on all my pushers, it's time to start making the collars. I tell Jack Nelson and Kelly that they've got to come right out of the stationhouse and back onto the street as soon as they've taken in a pusher. It's the only way to do a clean operation.

If they stay in the precinct, processing their prisoner, I'm left on my own on the street and that's the most dangerous time for me, when the arrests start. There's nine pushers to be picked up.

The first pusher I see is a little guy called Mario. I go back to the team, tell them where he is and give them a description. I slip back to where Mario is and I'm standing with a bunch of junkies nearby, outside a pizzeria, when I see Jack's car come roaring up. The team spots Mario, the car doors fly open and out come Jack Nelson and Kelly. All the junkies freeze.

The team picks Mario from off his feet and physically toss him into their car. Then they speed away . . . it's just like a kidnap. That does it . . . the foxes are in the chicken coop and the chickens are squawking.

"Hey, Mario's busted," one says. "It's the feds, I know it."

"Yeah," says another, "and he's dirty."

They look at each other and I know what they're thinking: There's got to be a rat around. Suddenly, they're all gone. It's like they're standing on a magic carpet and suddenly somebody pulls it away. They disappear that quick. I walk around and the word's gone ahead of me. Brook Avenue, St. Anne's Avenue, all the cross streets . . . they're all deserted, like a ghost town.

The next day, I'm back on the street and so is the team. Jack Nelson and Kelly arrest pusher after pusher. It looks good, it looks as if we'll make a clean sweep of all nine that I've doubled up on. But I make a couple of bad mistakes.

While I'm in the Blue Sea Restaurant, I see a couple we want, called Davey and Weasle. I telephone a drugstore where I know the team is waiting and I tell them this Davey and Weasle are in the restaurant. "We're on our way," Jack says.

Nelson and Kelly show up at the restaurant. They bust through the locked glass door and arrest three guys. They also find three ounces of pure heroin, which is being packaged in the restaurant, worth over $10,000 on the street. A crowd gathers across the street and I mingle with the junkies, watching what's going on at the restaurant. I shouldn't have done that . . . I should have stayed out of sight.

When the team leaves and goes back to the Precinct, I know they're finished. They're not going to come back on the street any more, because we'd agreed to end it with these last arrests. They've already got eight guys arrested.

But there's one more guy I want, Black Tony, one of the dudes who sells in the schoolyard. I haven't seen him yet.

I go to a drugstore to telephone the stationhouse and as I go, I get this feeling I'm being followed. It's just a feeling . . . I don't see anybody. It's after midnight. I talk to Jack and tell him to come out one more time so he can pick up Black Tony.

Jack is upset. "Tony," he says, "let's end this now. We can come back some other time for the last guy. The street is too hot and we got too much work here, processing our prisoners." He won't come out again.

"All right, Jack," I say, "you stay there and when I find him, I'll give you a call."

"No, Tony," he tells me, "you get back into the stationhouse. It's too dangerous for you to still be out in the street. I'm warning you now . . ."

But I won't listen to him. I hang up and go looking for Black Tony. There's not a soul on the street. I can hear my own footsteps like they're magnified and now the sweat is starting. I go up 137th Street and there's no sign of Black Tony, no sign of anybody, down 138th Street, up 139th Street, all he way up to 144th Street. There's no junkies, not even straight people.

I'm going west on 144th Street, heading for the schoolyard where I think I might still find Black Tony. Suddenly, from the darkness, I hear a voice.

"Hey, Solo," it says. It's a creepy, whining sort of a voice. I turn round and I see a dark figure behind me at the end of the block, maybe 50 yards away, on Brook Avenue. I look closer and I see there are three of them.

"Hey, Solo, come here, man," comes the voice out of the darkness. As he speaks, I see more guys join him until they're blocking the street behind me. In a line, they start walking towards me. "Oh, my God," I say to myself. I walk away, not fast . . . they're not coming fast either.

"Hey, Solo, come on, man," the voice says. "We're going to my pad and we're gonna shoot up. I got free junk for you. Come over here, baby. Let's go."

I'm so scared I can't even swallow . . . that's how bad it is. I'm like gulping for air and I have no strength. What the fuck am I going to do now? How the hell am I going to get out of this? I curse myself for staying on the street. I could have been home by now watching TV.

What puts the fear of God into me is that I see more guys blocking the other end of the street in front of me. There's no way out. They've got me cooped up in the block.

"Hey, Solo," comes that voice again, with a sort of giggle in it. I'm standing there, in the middle of the block, with them coming slowly at me from both ends. All of a sudden there's a shot.

I run to the sidewalk where there are three garbage cans and I get down behind them. Peering round the sides, I see these guys getting nearer . . . they're carrying clubs and pipes and I know one of them has a gun. More shots. From the sequence, I know there's at least three guns out there. They sound like .22s from the way they pepper the garbage cans and the brick of the building behind me.

Taking out my .38, I aim and fire. Bam! They don't expect that, I guess, and they scatter, jumping behind garbage cans and parked cars. It's straight out of my cowboys and Indians days, but this isn't any fun. "Oh, my God," I think, "I'll never get out of this." I fire again. They start pitching their clubs and pipes at me, as well as shooting the .22s.

I'm down to my last two shells, when I feel a burning sensation on the right cheek of my backside. I don't have time to check it because, praise-be-to-God, a yellow taxicab comes into the block. The driver can't know what's going on because he's going slow, just cruising as if he's looking for a fare. I decide to give him one.

As the cab gets close to me, I run out from behind the garbage cans. More shots . . . two, three, four. I dive right through the open back window of the cab as if the hounds of hell are after me, which they are. The cab driver doesn't know what's going on, but whatever it is, he doesn't like it.

As I get myself right side up, I see the punks running for the cab. "Jesus!" he says and he stops the cab. He looks round at me and he says, "Hey, get the fuck out of my cab."

"Move," I say, "these guys are after me. Move!"

"I don't want no part of all this," he says. He's pretty scared, but no more than me. "Get outta here," he yells.

"Yeah?" I say and I stick my gun at his head. "Drive or I'll blow your tonsils out. I mean it. Turn round and drive!" The gun makes up his mind for him. He puts the cab in gear and, zap, he drives full ahead, right through a bunch of punks who're coming for us from the front. Some shots and some sticks hit the cab but we get through them, with me still holding the gun to the driver's head.

"Is this a stickup?" the driver asks.

"It's no robbery . . . just go," I tell him.

When we get to 138th Street, I jump out of the cab and run. I run to the stationhouse and when I get there, what I've been through is too much for me. I collapse on the floor. I must have been some sight. Two cops think I'm some kind of a bum and they drag me to my feet. But Jack Nelson is there.

"Hold it," he says. "He's my buddy." And he takes me upstairs to the squad room.

One of the cops says, "Hey, he's bleeding," and I look down and there's a trail of blood behind me. It's dripping down my leg. I pull off my pants and there it is . . . I've been shot in the behind. A chunk of flesh has been nicked off.

Just then the cab driver I hijacked comes in to complain about it. Jack Nelson sits him down and tries to explain what it's all about, but the cab driver doesn't seem to believe him when he says I'm a cop. He's some kind of an ass. He won't believe a cop can be dressed like a bum and can stick a gun at his head and take over his cab. Finally, he takes off, but I can see he doesn't believe a word of it.

Now comes the brass. Because shots were fired, I have to be interviewed by sergeants, lieutenants, captains. I know it's necessary because you can't have cops wanging off shots all over the place, but it's still a drag, all the formalities. They're questioning, questioning, questioning and I'm doing my best to tell them all about it.

Bob Kelly, he looks at all this and he says, "Hey, shouldn't somebody get Tony into a hospital so he can be repaired? The guy's bleeding like a stuck pig." I am, too.

One of my superiors says, "Uh? Oh, yeah, better get an ambulance for him."

"No," says Bob, "I'll drive him in."

Mr. Clean takes me to Lincoln Hospital, which doesn't please me too much because that place is a real bucket of blood, a butcher house. But they clean the wound and put a bandage on it. It's a clean wound . . . it could have been a lot worse. What's more painful is my knees, which got scraped when I dived behind those garbage cans, but they're okay, too.

I don't telephone Helen, like Bob wants me to, because I don't want her all upset. She's had enough telephone calls about me being hurt and it doesn't do any good anyway.

The next day, I'm at home, spreading some fertilizer on my lawn where I've got a bad case of crab grass and dandelions. While I'm doing this, my mind is on the street and the gunfight. Across the way, a neighbor who works for the

IBM, a clerical man, he sees me and he calls across, "Hi, there, Tony. How're you doing?"

"Fine," I say. I look at him and the nice, clean houses with their neat lawns and gardens, and the blue sky with just a few fluffy white clouds, and the birds singing, and my kids just turning into the driveway, coming home from school. I look at it all. I'm just happy to be alive.

At times like this, I ask myself why the hell I should stay in this undercover work for more than nine years. But I know the answer.

In fact, there's more than one answer. When I first started undercover, I was excited because it meant getting out of uniform, and that was the ambition of every patrolman. More than that, it could lead to me being a detective, and to be a detective in the New York Police Department, that's the greatest. I guess a Scotland Yard detective feels the same.

Working undercover was the best way for me to win promotion, because I only have a basic education and you've got to do a lot of studying and passing examinations if you want to move up in other sections of the department.

Even so, as I got more experience and realized just how damned dangerous it was, some of the excitement drained away and I started wondering how long I could last without getting my throat cut. But it worked both ways. The longer I was undercover, the more valuable I became to the bosses. The longer it went on, the more recognition and medals I won. The longer I lasted, the more promotions I got. And that meant more money for Helen and the kids and the home in the suburbs.

Within three months of going undercover, I got my gold badge as a detective third grade. In a few more years, I got my second grade and then first grade. There aren't many cops who break through to first grade detective.

Also, in spite of the constant fear, there was an excitement still. My old boss, now retired, an Irish deputy chief inspector, said he made me his Guinea undercover cop because he was impressed with my eagerness. Well, I am an eager guy.

In my undercover days, when I got up in the morning and went to meet my team, when we headed for a junkie area and I knew I had to go in there alone, I was scared but I was also excited. They talk about guys who have a death wish. Maybe, I have an excitement wish.

There was the recognition that goes with a job like that. Other cops, they knew about me because of my work. Judges and lawyers in courts, they knew me and I've had a number of compliments from grand juries I've worked with. I liked that, the little feeling of being a celebrity.

That doesn't mean I didn't have my bad times. More than once, after I'd been cut or shot, I tossed my badge at my boss and said I wanted out. Just like the movies. But they always talked me round.

One of my back-up teams, they heard I was planning to get out of undercover work, which meant they would have to find another good undercover cop. They took me to a Chinese restaurant and they filled me with good food while they persuaded me to stay. I like Chinese food and they talked me round.

But, more than anything, it was my feelings about hoods and dope pushers that kept me going back on the street.

Why has some creep got to go out and rob another guy? Why has some scumbag got to sell dope? Why has some bastard got to go out and take advantage of somebody else when there's a guy, a father like mine, who worked so hard for so little and never hurt anybody? I get angry just thinking about it.

My dad was honest because that's the kind of guy he was.

He could have gone bad and put a lot of money in the bank like the Big Gees around the neighborhood. He wouldn't do it.

That's why I felt the way I did about criminals and muggers and dope pushers and thieves. Maybe that's why I took it personally. Maybe that's why I worked up to third grade detective, and then second grade and finally first grade detective.

In the back of my mind, these guys who make the easy bread by hurting other people, these bastards, they're my enemies and I fight all of them. I fight them hard because I know they laugh at anybody like my dad who doesn't steal and dies without any money in the bank.

Especially, I hate the goddam dope pushers. My father died of lung cancer because of the smoke he breathed in the factory he worked in during the last ten years of his life.

He worked under lousy conditions. He didn't break the law. You think I'm going to rest easy with these robbers, these pushers who never work and make the easy money?

Shit, no.

The team I worked with the most was Detective Stevie Wyatt and Detective John Toko, both sharp, aggressive guys, but both gentlemen. They were quiet, serious cops who had a very businesslike way about them. Unlike some detectives who've hit the headlines, they didn't use force unless they had to, although they could be tough when necessary.

These two, they gave me terrific cover. But, occasionally I got the impression they looked down on me because I was dressed in dirty old clothes and I was unshaven and I acted like a junkie. Sometimes, it was as though they thought of me as a real junkie.

One time, when we had to make some notes, I suggested

going to a restaurant, but they wouldn't do it. It happened again and I realized it was because they didn't want to be seen by decent people in my company. I put up with this since they were a great team to work with.

We start an operation in a Spanish area between Columbus Avenue and Amsterdam Avenue. There's so much junk being dealt there that the mayor's office closes a street, a block on 84th Street. I go in and I buy from more than twenty pushers. I don't even make a dent, it's that bad.

At this time, Wyatt and Toko have chipped in and bought a 1944 Plymouth to work in . . . a real old bomb they got for about $25 . . . so they won't have to use their own car.

The team parks near the area and we sit there, discussing how we're going to handle the buys and then the arrests. I'm wearing my tattered old clothes and my black beret. I'm carrying a large knife and one of my favorite weapons, a length of piano wire, to each end of which is attached a big nail spike, three or four inches long. It wraps up real small, but in an emergency I can bring it out and use it like a whip . . . it can cut off a guy's hand or permanently alter the expression on his face. Also, if you need to, you can tie up a guy's hands with this wire and he'll never free himself.

I go into this block and start making contacts with pushers. There's a guy I call Brown Jacket who has a little wisp of beard trailing down from his chin. I tell him I want to cop and he takes me to a building, something like the house of horrors, on West 85th Street. On the stoop is another pusher who I meet through Brown Jacket. He has a huge scar running down from his right eye to his neck . . . I call him Big Scar. With him is a guy called Johnny.

The team is parked on Central Park West and I go back to report on the situation. The back seat of the Plymouth is falling apart, with the springs coming through. I always have to sit in a hole, my ass resting on the floorboards . . . I feel as though I'm a foot shorter than them.

"Hey, Stevie," I say, "I don't want to sit on the floor no more. You understand?"

"Don't worry about it," Stevie says.

"I want to sit in the front," I say.

"You'll never sit in the front," he comes back. "The only time you'll sit in the front is when you change your clothes." I'm pissed off at his attitude, but there's nothing I can do. I need them because I know that a couple of other undercover cops who went into this block were taken apart. One of them had both his arms broken and the other was cut around the neck and fractured his ankle. They were put out of action.

In the next few days, I make more contacts, more buys. I go into one building on West 85th Street and then into the next building. They're both alive with pushers and junkies, just like the house of horrors. The hallways and corridors are full of junkies nodding off and pushers dealing. It's what they call a Casbah, with up to a hundred rooms on each floor. Every time I have to go in there, I'm sweating because I know any of these guys will embalm me. I tell the team to watch me constantly with the binoculars and when I'm inside one of the buildings for any length of time, I tell them they had better come charging in with the cavalry, bugles blowing.

The selling is so open that one guy, called Sapo, goes on the street advertising his wares. "Five-dollar bags!" he calls.

The average person living in New York City has no idea what goes on in the junkie areas. It's a new dimension . . . it's like going from land to water or from the ground to the air. Not even the cops know what it's like, except for the few guys who go undercover. This block on 85th Street, it's really cancerous. I have to become part of the scene.

In the Casbah, I move around, begging for a couple of dollars so I can get a fix. These guys wouldn't give me a quarter, not even a cigarette, let alone two dollars, but this way I can introduce myself into the background.

"Hey, man, I'm short," I'd say. "You put three dollars in with me and we'll go down together . . . I've got the cooker." Always the reply was the same.

"Get the fuck outta here." They're disgusted with me, but they believe I don't have any money so that makes it safer for me. I do it from floor to floor, making myself known. Among the junkies lying around and nodding off, I meet a couple of guys, one Italian and one Irish. The Italian guy comes from my neighborhood in East Harlem, but I don't know him because he's younger than me . . . we talk about Jefferson Park and Benjamin Franklin High School.

"Yeah," he says, "remember that teacher there, Mr. Key, that colored guy when they had riots there?" But mostly we talk about junk.

We talk about which heroin is good stuff, which is bad, which is a good pusher, which one sells bad stuff, where's a good place to rob. The Irish guy says, "Listen, I know a place we can go and get some money, but we need a third man. How about it?" If the addict has a code it's this: you got to get money, either from mugging, burglary, robbery or breaking into cars.

So when a junkie tells another junkie he knows how to make some money, the guy's got to go along with it or he'll be suspect. I can't afford that. I go along with them. They say that after they've broken into a car, they're going to buy either from Chino or Bobby. Okay, now I've got the names of two more pushers.

We go to West End Avenue and start looking into parked

cars, but this Irish guy knows where he's going. He takes us to 96th Street where there's a hotel and outside there's a blue Ford. On the back seat I see a suitcase, two cameras, a tape recorder and a typewriter. This owner deserves what he's going to get. He's stupid to leave all that stuff in his car like that . . . no matter where he is in the fifty states. You don't leave anything in your car, not even in Alaska.

They want me to keep a lookout while they work on the car. I'm on the corner when I see a patrol car coming slowly into the intersection. I run to them and I whistle a warning.

They move away and sit on the stoop until the patrol car has gone by. Then they go back to work . . . it only takes them two minutes to put a wire through the crack in the door and lift up the knob of the door lock. They open the door, remove the items, quietly close the door and walk away. Not even running.

We go back to the Casbah. We check over the goods and then the two guys say they're going off to sell them. I say, "Fine," and they smile at each other because they have no intention of letting me in on the money they make. When they've gone to their fence, I go to the team and tell Wyatt and John Toko about it. They take off to try and grab the two guys for possession of stolen goods. They miss them, though.

Later, through the Irish and the Italian guy, I meet Chino and Bobby, the two pushers they were talking about. I double up my buys on Chino, who's a mean fuck, in the same day. An hour or so later, all the junkies are inside one of the buildings because it's raining, and I'm pretending to nod off on the second floor hallway.

All of a sudden, I hear a guy screaming on the floor below me and when I look down I see Chino with about three of his pals. They're attacking a junkie. The three guys hold this junkie while Chino punches him in the face and then in the belly. Chino steps back, pauses for a moment and then he kicks him in the balls. The guy goes down.

Chino reaches into his pocket and pulls out a K-55, a knife you can buy for about fifty cents. He opens up the knife and looks down at the junkie, who is lying face down clutching his groin. Chino slashes him down the back from neck to buttocks. The blade goes right through the junkie's clothes and there's a spurt of blood. I almost puke. I have to get out of there.

I go down and I have to step over this guy's body. Chino's still there, with the knife in his hands. I know this pusher doesn't like me.

"Hey, man," he says, "you wanna cop?"

"I just did it with you," I say. "I don't have no money."

"Where did you shoot up?" he wants to know.

"Upstairs," I tell him.

"Where upstairs?" This Chino is suspicious of me. But I give him some bullshit story that I did it on the roof. I manage to get out. I run back to the team and tell them about the stabbing.

"Stevie," I say, "you've got to take this guy off the street. You've got to. Otherwise, I know he means trouble for me." They agree.

That night, I go back to the building, looking for Chino so I can tell the team where to find him. He's on the first floor. I go to the team.

I give a description of Chino, adding, "Stevie, he's dirty right now. Go get him." Off they go, but Chino has vanished. The problem is that the Casbah always has a lookout guy and whenever cops come by, the warning is passed before they can make a collar.

I go back into the buildings. I go up through one onto the roof and down through the other. Chino's nowhere around.

209

I hunt through the streets, but nobody knows where Chino is. He must know it's hot. Then, all of a sudden, I see him going into another building on West 85th Street. I follow him, right behind. He spots me.

"What d'you want, motherfucker?" he says.

"You got dope?" I ask.

"No, I got nothing. Get the hell outta here. I see you later on Broadway, junkie." We're inside the building now. I've got to take him. I reach into my pocket and feel the length of piano wire with the nails at each end and I smile at him.

"Okay," I say, "I'll see you on Broadway." When he turns away from me, about to go up the stairs, I wrap the piano wire around his throat. When thin wire like that goes around your throat, it digs into your skin. No matter what you do, your fingers can't get that wire out of your throat.

Slowly, I bring him down to the floor and I tie his throat to the banister of the stairway. He can't do anything. He's trying to pull the wire from his neck, but he can't do it.

I run. I run real fast all the way to the team.

"Stevie," I say, "I got this guy, Chino. He's wired up to a banister on West 85th Street. Get there quick!" They screech off, going through lights, and at the house they find Chino still trying to get the wire from around his neck. They make the arrest. Beautiful. They have to get a pair of pliers to cut the wire from around his neck. I think I was the only guy who used this piano wire technique. It was great because it took up no room, but it made perfect handcuffs, as well as a weapon.

In a month, I buy from eleven different pushers in the Casbah. I'm shitting every time I go in there and I'm glad when we decide it's time to make the collars on the pushers I've doubled up on. One of the pushers we have to take is Big Scar. He's easy. He's standing in front of the building when

Wyatt and Toko pull up in their beat-up old Plymouth. Without a word, not a goddam word, they cuff him and put him in the back seat so he's sitting in the hole where I have to sit when I'm with the team. The thing about Wyatt and Toko is that they don't look like cops . . . they look more like insurance brokers, very businesslike.

Sometimes, when they hunt for my pushers, I'm sitting in that back seat. On my head I've got a cardboard carton with slits cut in it so that I can look out but nobody can see who I am. Or I wear a weird-looking mask which gives me a complete disguise. Of course, I wear clothes different to those I wear on the street.

We drive along the street with me peering out so that I can point to the pushers. When the team arrests them, the pushers find themselves sitting next to a freaky-looking guy with a box on his head, or a mask, and they desperately try to make out who it is that's fingered them. "Who the hell is it?" they would ask themselves, but I'm not about to help them. Nor is the team.

As they pick up the pushers, the word goes round that the block is hot and all the action goes indoors. I want Brown Jacket because he's a big seller, but the team has trouble reaching him. He's keeping a lookout of the window on the second floor and every time Wyatt and Toko show up, he vanishes. Three times I tell the team where Brown Jacket is and three times when they go into the building, he's gone.

When we meet, the team and me, Stevie says, "Screw you, Tony. The guy's not there." I tell them to wait. I go back and there he is, the scumbag, back on the second floor, looking out the window. I'm thinking, I'll take this bastard myself if he's alone, but there's three or four junkies with him. I go into the backyard, thinking that maybe there's some back entrance Wyatt and Toko can use to sneak up on him without him seeing them.

It's all fences . . . no way for the team to get into the building. I see something else, though. As I'm walking back through the hallway, I see a bunch of kids have started a fire with garbage and an old mattress just inside the back door. It's mostly smoke, but then flames start leaping up. In another couple of minutes, it's too hot to even get close to and the kids run off. I race off to turn in an alarm. While I'm doing this, I'm thinking, maybe this is my chance.

I run full speed to Wyatt and Toko. I'm panting when I get there. "Stevie," I gasp, "get ready. There's gonna be firemen at that building in a couple of minutes. There's gonna be all sorts of confusion. That bum is still up on the second floor. When the firemen go in, you go in. He won't spot you in all the panic."

Stevie looks at me, smiles and shakes his head. We can hear the sirens. I run back to watch. Lots of smoke is coming from the Casbah. The first fire truck pulls up and out come the firemen with their hoses. Up come Wyatt and Toko, right after the firemen. They plunge into the house and, zap, up to the second floor. Brown Jacket is hanging out of the window staring down at all the commotion of fire trucks and hoses and helmeted firefighters. He turns round to say something to the other junkies about the fire, and there's the team.

They grab him and walk him out through the firemen, who've soon got the blaze under control. Beautiful. Absolutely beautiful. Stevie Wyatt and John Toko, they're still smiling when they put Brown Jacket in the car. Me, I'm grinning from ear to ear.

Stevie starts calling me "firebug," but, of course, I didn't start the fire. It was those kids. I'm just lucky, I guess.

13

PEOPLE move out of the city to escape crime. Parents think that out in the suburbs, with all the green lawns and pretty trees, Junior won't start taking drugs. But there's no escape. There's heroin and cocaine and pot out in Suffolk County and Nassau County and Westchester County, just like there is on 125th Street.

That's why my bosses call me in and tell me I have to break in a deputy sheriff from Westchester County. I've got to show him how an undercover detective operates so that he can make use of the expertise up on his turf in the suburbs. He's a nice guy, this Pete Carbo, about twenty-one, good-looking and real solid about the shoulders. When I first see him, I think he's wearing shoulder pads like the football players wear, but it's muscle. I look at him and think, this dude's going to be the healthiest-looking junkie New York City's ever seen.

I'm pissed off when I'm assigned to Pete because I don't like working with a partner . . . it always ends up shitty. But my bosses, they tell me I've got to do it, and, of course, I have to. They give me a back-up team, one of them Rocco Milit, who happens to be a neighbor of mine.

Rocco's something. He's about 6 feet and 200 pounds. His

brow protrudes from his head, and his eyebrows, they meet over his nose in a single bar of hair. He looks like something from the Stone Age—those guys who drag their broads back to their cave by the hair.

He isn't like most other detectives. He hardly ever chastises a suspect . . . he doesn't have to because he's so fearsome-looking. When he approaches a pusher, the pusher gapes at him in horror and immediately reaches into his pocket to hand over the stuff. The pusher is sure this brute is going to kill him.

But, tough as Rocco looks, he is in fact a very compassionate man. He doesn't like violence, although he can be tough when he's got to fight. His wife, she's in complete control of him and of their seven kids. She treats him like a baby . . . in fact, she reprimands Rocco more than she does her kids. When Helen and I meet Rocco's wife, she says, "Tsk, tsk, what am I gonna do with Rocco? He's like a baby. He gets underfoot all the time." I'm glad they give me Rocco to work with because he's aggressive on the street and he doesn't mind long hours.

We decide to go undercover at 180th Street on the West Side, around Audubon Avenue, so I can start breaking in this kid Pete.

We hang around awhile and pretty soon I make a contact with a young guy called Pancho, who offers to sell us some grass. That's good enough as openers for young Pete so he can learn how these things are done. This Pancho tells us to be outside a store on Aububon Avenue an hour later and his connection will be there. Okay. Pete's excited that we've made a hit.

When we go to this store, there's an old man sitting in front. He's short, wearing a brown fedora and he's unshaven. As we approach him, he smiles at us.

"I know why you here," he says. "You wait. Pancho and Johnny, they coming right back." And he keeps smiling at us. I ask him about the grass, but he won't say anything. He just smiles. He's weird.

A few minutes later, up the block comes Pancho with another young guy who's wearing a black hat . . . this must be Johnny.

"How much you want?" this Johnny asks.

"Give me an ounce, for now," I say.

"You give me $25," he says. I give it to him and he counts it. Then he puts it in his pocket and walks away. I call after him, "Hey, Johnny . . . what about the stuff?"

"That's okay," he says over his shoulder. "He'll take care of you." And he points at the old man sitting in front of the store. I go over to the old man, who says, "Follow me."

He leads us over to the corner of the street and the old man reaches down under the fender by the right front wheel. He comes up with a brown paper package and out of this he takes an envelope which he gives me. He's about to walk away when I ask him if I can get more later.

"You come back any time . . . we take care of you," he says.

After he's gone, I try to explain to Pete some of the little things you have to watch out for when you're doing this sort of undercover stuff. I point out to him that we've got three defendants in this one buy, because Pancho, Johnny and the old man are all involved in the sale of the grass. Pancho is the steerer, Johnny is the connection and the old man is the flunky who has the stuff in his possession. I tell Pete that now we've got to double up on them.

I tell him something else. "Pete," I say, "don't ever leave me on my own. Always follow me. Now, even if I tell you I'm going off to make a buy with someone, you've gotta refuse to let me go on my own. This is important. I might tell you to stay where you are and wait for me. Don't do it. Insist on coming with me. Got it?" He says he understands. I tell him other things, but I make a big deal out of this question about him leaving me because if I have to go into a hallway or an apartment to make a buy, I want Pete with me. After you've worked on the street a while, you get an instinct for something like this.

The point is that I want to work on my own. That's how I got the name Tony Solo, and I'm proud of it. But if I'm assigned to a partner, then we've got to work together, and that means you never split up. It can mean trouble.

The next day, we're back on Audubon Avenue and 181st Street. It's a beautiful, sunny afternoon with the kids running home from school. There's a young guy on the corner who's got something wrong with his nose. It's dripping and he keeps touching it and spitting into the gutter. I say to him, "Hey, man, what's happened to your nose?" He says it happens while he's burglarizing an apartment. The owner wakes up and this kid has to dive through a window to escape. His nose gets busted, but he can't go to a hospital because of the circumstances and he sets the bone himself, which doesn't work too well and now he's got this trouble with it.

I ask him if he's seen Johnny, because I want to cop some grass.

"His stuff is garbage," he says. "If you want boss stuff, I've got it. I can get you Panamanian Red . . . the best."

"How much is an ounce?"

"I can get it for you for $15, maybe $20 at the most." That's a good deal anywhere, I think. I tell this kid I'll buy some. But as we're talking, we suddenly hear a scream.

We look round and we see a tall, young guy with blond

hair running down the street, being chased by a small, black-haired man. This man has a knife and he's also got a very mean face. When they're near us, the fellow with the knife catches up with the young guy and grabs him by his blond hair. All of a sudden he starts plunging his knife into the kid, who's already screaming. The knife cuts into his arms and then it goes right into his belly and the kid goes down, clutching his middle. The little guy hasn't had enough. He starts knifing the fellow on the ground in his thighs and buttocks, slashing at his face as well. He's kicking him, too.

This all happens in a couple of seconds, it seems like. The little guy then wipes his blade on the clothes of the wounded kid and starts walking slowly towards us. It's as though he's saying, have we got any objections?

I whisper to Pete, "Don't say nothing." But Pete is all upset. He wants to go and help the kid. I have to grab him by the arm and snarl at him, "Don't move an inch, not one inch!"

The pusher we're with . . . his name turns out to be Ralphie . . . he joins in, "Yeah, man, that's Bruno. He's wild. He killed two guys. Don't say nothing." We just stand there. Bruno looks us over, seems satisfied and turns back. He throws another kick at the head of the guy who's groaning on the ground and walks slowly away up the block.

An ambulance and the cops turn up and the wounded guy is taken to a hospital. I learn later that he won't tell the cops why he's attacked like that, because he'd cheated Bruno in a narcotics deal. After it's all over, up comes Pancho and Johnny, and I agree to make a $25 buy. It's like before. Johnny takes the money and walks away while Pancho reaches into his shirt and hands me a brown envelope. Johnny never handles the stuff himself, just the money.

217

The first guy, Ralphie, he says he'll take us to his connection, but I say we have to go and get some more money. He says he'll wait for us.

As we're walking away, I tell Pete, "Listen, when you're on the street working, you're not a cop . . . you're a junkie. If you'd done anything back there, you'd have blown the whole thing." But Pete is real upset by the action, the knifing and all the blood on the street. For that matter, so am I.

"That guy was almost killed," he says.

"Yeah, and if we'd done anything, we'd have been in the same boat," I say. "If we tried anything, they'd all have been on us. To them, we're not cops . . . we're street people, and they'd treat us the same way. When you're undercover, playing a junkie, you've got to be a junkie."

Even so, we're both shook up by the whole thing, and to tell the truth, if it had gone any further I'd probably have done something.

Later, we go back to see Ralphie with the dripping nose, and he's on the same corner. He wants to know if we have the money and we say yes. Off we go to find his connection. We walk all over, ending up at 191st Street and St. Nicholas Avenue. Man, am I tired.

"This is it," Ralphie says. "But only one guy comes in. He [pointing to Pete] can stay outside." I give Pete a hard look to remind him about not leaving me. He gets it.

"Oh, no," he says, "I'm following my money."

"You ain't coming in," Ralphie says.

"No, you wait outside," I say, not meaning it, of course.

"I'm coming in," Pete says. Good boy. I pretend to plead with him.

"I'm not gonna take off with your money," I say. "I'll be right back." Now Pete fucks up. I could kick him.

"Okay," he says. "I'll wait here."

I think, what the hell, he'll follow me into the building anyway because of what I told him. Ralphie and I, we leave Pete outside and go up to the fourth floor. I'm not too worried because I'm sure Pete will have snuck in after us. Ralphie knocks on a door but there's no answer. He knocks again and still no answer.

"He must be at the store," he says. "Let's go."

I make a bad mistake. I turn and I go down the stairs ahead of Ralphie. I should never have done that. Never. Almost immediately I feel a punch . . . that's what it seems like . . . in my right lower back. Then Ralphie's arm comes round my throat and he puts a knife to my head while he drags me down to the ground. When I'm down, he pricks my throat with his knife . . . he punctures the skin.

"Give me the money," he says. "Give it to me, you bastard. I'll kill you. I'll do worse than what Bruno did to that white kid on the street."

"Wait a minute," I gasp. "I can't talk."

He's kneeling over me. The knife is against my throat.

"Give me the fucking money," he yells.

"It's in my shoes," I say. He makes me reach down and pull the money out of my shoes. Then he takes my wallet. He gets about $100 in all. While this is going on, I realize that punch I felt was really Ralphie stabbing me. I can see blood on the stairs and I'm beginning to feel weak. I'm shit scared because now I know what Ralphie's going to do. He's going to stab me again, enough to put me out of action, to stop me chasing him or yelling for Pete. Maybe he'll kill me. I'm on my own and he can do anything he likes.

"Hey, Ralphie," I say, "wait a minute, man. I don't care about the bread. Take it."

"Fuck you," he says. He looks wild.

"Just leave me a dollar," I plead. "Leave me enough to get home. I'll tell the guy downstairs that you took me off and that'll be the end of it. But if you stab me again, we'll both be back to look for you."

"Get up," he says, and he grabs my collar, the knife still at my throat, and hauls me to my feet. I'm helpless with that knife there. I can't use karate on him . . . nothing. He drags me up to the next floor, near the roof.

"Listen, pal," I say, "don't get excited. All you got to do is tie me up and then run. Then I can't follow you." He likes that idea.

"Give me your belt," he says. I take it off and all the time I'm thinking, where the hell is Pete? The blood is oozing out of my back. It's all because I'm working with a partner, I think. If Pete hadn't been around, I'd never have come into the building with this Ralphie. Christ, why won't they let me work solo?

Ralphie takes my thick leather belt and starts to try and tie my hands. To do this, he has to take the knife from my throat.

This is the one chance I'm going to get. The only one. I step back and I kick him right in the gut. He goes reeling back across the hallway and bounces off the wall. He comes back at me with his knife and I throw a punch at his chest which sends him back again. He takes my belt, wraps it around his fist and starts lashing me in the face with it. He closes my left eye so I can't see properly. I'm getting weak, very weak.

He comes at me again with the knife. I grab his knife hand with both my hands and we struggle, me trying to keep the knife away, him trying to slash my throat. Because I'm leak-

220

ing blood, I'm weaker than he is, but I manage to kick him in the groin, not hard but enough to knock the wind out of him. I'm exhausted and I sink down to the floor. While he's still trying to get his breath back, I reach inside my waistband and I pull out my gun. I point it at him.

Ralphie sees it and he's shocked. He can't understand where the gun comes from.

"Listen, Ralphie," I say, "I'm a cop. You just stabbed a cop. Drop the knife."

"Drop the knife, shit!" he says. "I'm gonna kill you, motherfucker!"

He starts towards me and that's when I do it. One shot.

He grunts and he drops as hard as if he's jumped off a 10-foot wall. That's how fast he goes down. I get up and I scream down the stairs for Pete. I think at the least he's down in the hallway, but he's not. He's still outside. People living in the building start coming out and I tell them to go and get Pete.

He comes running up and I say, "Pete, first things first. Get the team and get an ambulance." I'm having trouble talking and I have to lean against the wall. Pete has his gun in his hand, a .25 automatic, but there's no need for it now. He tells me to take it easy and he races off down the stairs, his gun still in his hand. We're both dressed like hippies and he's got a wisp of a beard. We both look undesirable.

He goes running down the street, looking for the team, the gun still in his hand. A patrol car is nearby and the cops spot him. It must have been some sight, this wild-looking hippie running through the streets with a gun in his hand. The cops pounce on him and cuff him. He tries to tell them who he is and what's happened, but they don't believe him. Seeing what he looked like, you can't blame them.

But the team sees all the activity in front of the building, cops called by people living in the building, and they zap up. They come running up the stairs and find me lying there in a pool of blood.

Ralphie's lying next to me and he doesn't look good, either. Cops start pouring up the stairs like housewives at a department store sale. They get us down, me coming last helped by Rocco Milit and an inspector. I feel as though I'm going to throw up. Out in the street, there's a crowd of 100 spectators or more, and when they see me being held, they think I'm a prisoner. That sets them off . . . they're ready to mob the cops.

"Pigs!" they start screaming. "They got one of our guys . . . look what they're doing to him. They beat him up."

Just then, a little boy comes up behind me and says, "Hey, look, he's all blood." And he lifts up my T-shirt to look closer. The cops chase away this kid and I look over my shoulder, down at my back. When I see the open wound and all the blood, that's it. I faint.

In the hospital, where I'm being sewed up, I find I'm in the same emergency room as Ralphie, who's also being worked on. I see this nurse, consoling this scumbag that tried to kill me. "Oh, you poor thing," she's saying, stroking his forehead. "Such a young man! What a sin."

She turns to me and says, "You're a cop? You're supposed to be a protector of the innocent? Is this what you do? You ought to be ashamed of yourself." I'll never forget it. This nurse, if that young punk got her in the dark, he'd mug her without a second thought.

She's not the only stupid person around. Some dopey patrolman calls my wife at home and says I'm laid out at the hospital. He gives her the impression I'm on a cold slab. She doesn't cry or anything. Her family drives her down to the hospital, and when she comes in and sees me alive, not badly hurt, being sewed up . . . that's when she starts crying. I'd like to find that patrolman and tell him what I think of him.

When the doctors have finished, I go home and Ralphie goes to a prison hospital. He's indicted on charges of attempted murder, robbery, assault and resisting arrest. After he's back on his feet, he applies for bail and they give it to him. He then jumps bail and takes off. They never do catch him to this day.

Pete Carbo . . . I ask him why he let me go in the building alone. He said I'm so convincing when I say he should stay behind, I do such a good acting job, that he thinks that's what I really want. It's an easy mistake if you're new to the street, and I tell him I understand. He's a good guy.

Later, Rocco Milit and me go back to the area and we round up Pancho and Johnny. The only one we never find is the old man. He's old but he's smart.

That's not the end of it. My boss writes to the commissioner, recommending I should get departmental recognition.

Sometime later, I'm told I've won the Combat Cross. Jesus. The only thing higher is the Medal of Honor, and usually you're dead when you get that one. I'm so excited, I could bust. Not bad for a Guinea cop.

I have to go down to City Hall to be presented with the medal by the mayor, John Lindsay. The ceremony is being held in the morning and I'm at the hospital all night with my mother, who's sick, so I have to change into my newly pressed uniform which I hardly ever wear, but there's no time and I have to change in the car going downtown.

Helen's with me, of course, and I give her my small off-duty gun to put in her handbag so it won't spoil the line of my smart uniform. Lindsay's real nice at the ceremony. When I walk up to him to receive the medal, he looks at the other decorations on my chest and he smiles and says, "You know, Detective Schiano, I don't think you have any more room for another medal on your chest." I mumble something and he finds a place and pins it on.

It's beautiful . . . except for one thing. While this is all going on, I'm thinking about my father and how proud he would be to see me standing in front of the mayor of New York City, getting a medal. If only he was alive, this guy who used to follow me on the streets when I was a patrolman, who always told me, "You be good boy, Anthony," who waved to me from the top of that water tower when I was in heli- copters.

The mayor invites us all down to his private office so he can meet the families of the cops who are getting awards. I introduce Helen to Lindsay and he puts his hand out to shake hers. "You must be very proud of your husband," he says, smiling. "Yes," she says, and just then she drops her handbag with my gun in it on the floor, almost on the mayor's foot. Luckily, it's not loaded.

The mayor bends down to pick it up; at the same moment Helen bends down and their foreheads bump together. Helen says later that it's really something, to be staring into Lind- say's eyes from that close range. She's tickled pink, in fact.

When we leave City Hall, we drive up the West Side to get onto the George Washington Bridge. I look out at the streets and I see some junkies standing on a corner, waiting for a connection. I know there's just as many addicts around as when I first went on the street . . . in fact, there's more. It's just the same . . . the newspapers blowing in the gutters, the garbage spilling out of the cans, the stinking hallways, the greasy basements, and the guys looking for a fix. I wonder if it'll be the same in another ten years' time. Or worse. The car moves on past the junkies and we go on home.

14

ALL cops have their favorite restaurants. One of my places is Joe and Joe's Restaurant at Castle Hill and Bruckner Boulevard in the Bronx. They make a bit of a fuss over me in there and that's okay by me.

The night of January 13, 1970, I was through with the undercover work and assigned to Eighth District Robbery. My partner Eddie Dillon and me, we decided to take a break and go get some dinner in Joe and Joe's. While I was eating my linguini spaghetti and calamare, I didn't know that I was just about to get a case that would take me nearly two years to break and cost me a lot of aggravation.

As we sat there, I told Eddie, a real Irish meat and potatoes guy, about the addition I was planning for my home up in the suburbs. I was going to have a big room off the kitchen with a cathedral ceiling and a stone fireplace. I knew where I could get the lumber cheap. Eddie, he's a sports nut. He listened to me going on about my house, but I knew he was more interested in the Super Bowl, so I let him talk about that for a while.

When we've finished eating, we go out and get into our unmarked black Ford to start patrolling again, Eddie at the wheel, me alongside him. The district includes the 41st, 43rd and 45th Precincts. We're driving north on Bruckner Boulevard when the radio starts making noises.

"Eighth District Robbery Squad," it says.

I pick up the microphone and reply, "Eighth District Robbery."

"A past 10–30, a past 10–30," Central says. "The location is East Tremont Avenue and Bruckner Boulevard."

"10–4," I say. "We're responding." That's the start of it all.

Eddie spins the wheel and puts his foot down. It isn't very dramatic because the best that car can do is about 50 m.p.h. It's a real load of nothing. Like most of our equipment, the best you can say about it is that it works. While Eddie is bulling his way through the traffic, I'm picking at the stuffing which is sticking up through a hole in the front seat.

We get to the location and find it's the Crosstown Diner, which is on a service road off Bruckner Boulevard. Three patrol cars with revolving beacons are already there. We get out and start scouting up the facts. When we put them all together, it comes out like this:

A truck driver named James Wilson, who worked for the Gamache Trucking Company in Fall River, Massachusetts, parked his rig outside the diner while he went in to get a meal.

When he came out, he found two men waiting for him. They stuck a gun in his ribs and made him hand over the keys to his truck, which was filled with 1,160 cases of Budweiser beer. The punks tossed the keys to a third man who appeared, and this third guy climbed up behind the wheel of the truck.

While he was doing this, the first two guys made Wilson get into the back of their car and kneel on the floor in the

227

back. One guy was at the wheel of the car, the other was in the back with the truck driver.

But things started to go wrong for the hijackers. An off-duty patrolman, Joe Kinsella, was driving by while all this was happening and he saw enough to become suspicious. When the punks' car drove away, this Kinsella followed in his car. He couldn't catch them and he gave up the chase. But he had scared the shit out of the punks and their car crashed into a snowbank on Pelham Parkway. Leaving Wilson in the back, they jumped out and took off on foot into the darkness.

About a block away from the diner, we can see the beer truck parked outside a men's hairdressing salon. We figure the third punk panicked when he saw his pals being chased and he must have abandoned the truck and taken off.

Eddie Dillon and me, we go through the routine. We take this truck driver, Wilson, who's arrived back at the diner, and we go check the punks' auto.

It's lying off Pelham Parkway on a snow-covered mall, its doors still open. We can see footprints the punks left, and in the back seat we find a .22 caliber starter's pistol. We take a note of the license plate and the vehicle inspection number, then we follow the footprints to a sidewalk that's been cleared of snow. We start the shitty part of being a detective, pounding the sidewalks and questioning people, questioning, questioning. All through this case, I'm throwing questions around and not getting enough answers.

We try stores and bars and apartment houses, but nobody saw anything. Finally, we come to a bar called the Tik Tok, on Wilkinson Avenue. It's not the sort of place you'd take your best girl, or even your second best, but at least it's warm. I'm taking it all in when a short guy, built something like a refrigerator, spots me and comes rolling over.

"Tony!" he says, all excited. "Jesus, it's good to see you."
He gives me a big hug which, normally, I wouldn't appreciate, but with this guy it's okay. It's Bo, my pal from the old days when I was growing up on East 114th Street. Now he's got something to do with running this bar, the Tik Tok.

After we've gone through the "long time, no see," stuff, I ask Bo if he's heard anything about the hijack, if he's seen anything of the two punks who took off.

Negative. Bo has done five years on a narcotics rap and I'm a cop, so things aren't the way they used to be. Even though we were kids together, I don't trust him any more than he trusts me. Just because Bo says he doesn't know anything about the screwed-up hijack, that doesn't mean I believe him.

Eddie Dillon and me, we go back to the 45th Precinct and later we get a fingerprint report. Nothing. The registration plate on the abandoned car, it turns out to belong to a Wallace Hinch of Bayside, Queens. But the National Crime Information Center says the plate goes with a 1956 Buick, not the white Chevrolet the hijackers used.

The vehicle inspection number is registered to a John Stern in Brooklyn. While we're digging up this information, I get a visitor at the Precinct. He identifies himself as Agent Brooks of the FBI . . . the case involves interstate trucking, which is an FBI matter. This agent, he takes the information he needs, but he doesn't seem particularly interested in it. He leaves and that's the last I see or hear of him. The hell with him.

The next day Eddie and me are supposed to be off duty, but we come in anyway so we can keep on top of the hijack case. The patrolman Kinsella, who chased the punks, telephones us.

He wants to know how we're getting on and he says he

could identify at least two of the hijackers if he should see them again. Things look good. We've got two solid witnesses and we've got two names, the owner of the registration plate and the owner of the vehicle inspection number. We drive out to Bayside, Queens, to have a chat with this Hinch.

We knock on the door and a slim woman in her thirties answers it. I tell her we want to talk to her husband. She stares at me and she says, "Wallace? You want to talk to Wallace? My husband is dead six months."

There goes one of our suspects. "Oh, shit!" I say, but that's to myself. To her I say, "Gee, I'm sorry to hear that." I tell her about the hijack and kidnap and I ask her what happened to her husband's car. More important, I ask about the license plate. She says she doesn't know anything about it. I ask her if her husband had any particular friends when he was alive. She comes up with one, a Dominic Capon, and she gives me his address and telephone number.

Eddie and me head back for the Bronx. At the tollgate on the Throgs Neck Bridge, we discover we don't have the metal plate saying "Police" which gets you through the tollgate for nothing.

Eddie sticks his head out of the window and he says to the tollkeeper, "Police." This tollkeeper, he's an old fart with a bulbous red nose like Rudolph the reindeer. He looks at us in our civilian clothes and he looks at our mud-spattered, beat-up, sad-looking car and he gets very sarcastic. "Sure, the commissioner and his deputy," he says. "That'll be twenty-five cents."

Eddie looks at me and he grins. "Hey, Tony," he says, "this guy don't believe we're cops. Shall we give him the quarter?" I decide this tollkeeper is just being obnoxious and we should prove we're cops to his complete satisfaction. We tell him to come closer to the car. Then I press the constant siren button. The car's not much, but the siren's okay. It starts wailing like a mad thing.

"Go, Eddie, go!" I yell, and Eddie puts his foot down. We look back and we see the tollkeeper's jaw drooping in astonishment and we see his hat's fallen on the ground. Wise guy. He believes we're cops now.

I give all the time I can to this hijack case, but in the South Bronx it's not like it appears in the detective books or in the movies. In the Eighth District, we get something like 4,000 robberies reported each year and that's too many for a cop to concentrate on one in particular. A detective in the South Bronx is overwhelmed with cases. The only reason there aren't even more is that there's not that much to steal in the South Bronx.

There's a constant stream of complaints of muggings, hold-ups, pocketbook snatchings, and so on. Like one that comes up while I'm trying to push the hijack investigation. I'm on an 8 A.M. to 4 P.M. duty and I'm just about ready to go home when a woman comes into the squad room looking like she tried to tackle a Mack truck. She's some mess. Her face is distorted so bad you don't want to look at it. Her left eye is closed and it's surrounded by blue and black marks. Covering her forehead is a big bandage and there's blood spattered on her hair and all over her dress. Her mouth is puffed up to twice the ordinary size. She's got dirt all over her clothes.

You see a victim like this and you think about the way the courts deal with the punks who do this sort of thing and, shit, you get angry. All the sympathy is for the punk . . . there's none left over for the hard-working guy who gets stabbed before he can take his pay packet home, none left for the woman who gets mugged. The courts make deals with criminals and pat their wrists and send them back to the streets so they can do the same thing all over again. Cops, like me, we see all this going on and it's a wonder more of us don't quit in disgust.

This woman, she was about sixty, she ran a check-cashing office. People who didn't have bank accounts went to her and she cashed their checks in return for a small sum of money.

She was taking the day's receipts to the bank from her office at Simpson Street and 163rd Street, when a young guy approached her. He grabbed her around the throat and, in broad daylight, dragged her into an alleyway. There were other people around and the woman was screaming.

This punk tried to grab her purse, but it had a strap which was around her shoulder and he couldn't get it off her. He started punching her in the face and she went down. Even then, he was still punching her. He took out a knife and he slashed her across the forehead. He was cursing her, but he still couldn't get the purse because the strap was twisted around the woman's body.

People in the street started to come over and the punk saw them and he took off, still without the purse. The woman lost consciousness but the people helped her and when she came round, one witness who wouldn't give her name said she knew the punk. She even knew his address . . . Simpson Street.

In the squad room, the check-cashing woman tells me all this and she gives me a description of the mugger. He's about eighteen, he's got a mustache and he's got short hair combed to the front. Better still, she says he's got a scar on his throat because she knows she left a deep scratch mark there. On top of that, she has a name.

I tell Eddie Dillon, "Eddie, come on, we've got a

grounder." That's what we call an easy arrest . . . a description, an address and a name. We go round to Simpson Street and we knock on the door of the apartment where this punk is supposed to live. There's no answer at first, but we keep knocking and eventually, an old woman comes. I can hear noise inside and I know there's more people there.

Through a crack in the door, near the hinges, I can see a young guy standing in nothing but pants. When I look closer, I see he's got a blade in his hand. Behind the old woman, four or five guys appear. I look at them and I know what they are. They're all junkies.

Eddie Dillon and me, we push our way further in, while the old woman starts demanding to know what we want. We're in a long, narrow hallway. The woman is in front of us and the junkies are behind her. To my left is this kid with the knife. It's not the sort of situation where you start advising people of their rights.

I turn to the punk with the knife and I ask, "What's your name?" He doesn't say anything, but the woman, his mother, I guess, does more than enough talking. She starts yelling at us. It's dark in the hallway and I can't see well. I reach in my pocket and I pull out a flashlight and I shine it at this kid's throat. Before I see anything else, I see he's freaked out on drugs. He's a mean-looking sonofabitch.

On his throat, I spot this scar and I know this is the guy. "Eddie," I say, "we got him," and as I say this, before the punk can bring up his knife, I throw him a punch right in his jaw. As he staggers back, the other guys jump Eddie. It's getting hot for both of us. The punk comes back at me with his knife. I whip out my gun and I smash him across the forehead with it. He goes down for good. I take his knife and turn. Eddie is having problems.

The woman's in my way and I can't get past her to help

my partner. She's screeching in Spanish. "Get out of my way, you bitch," I yell, but she won't budge. There's no other way . . . I give her a left hook to the jaw, not hard, but hard enough to move her so I can go help Eddie. The other guys see me coming with my piece and now Eddie's got his gun out, too, and they decide it's too much for them. They scatter, some through the door, some back into the apartment.

We pick up the punk, cuff him and drag him out to our car, where we throw him in the back seat. Back at the 41st Precinct, we call the woman who got mugged and she comes round with her sister. When the sister sees the punk, she takes her purse and she bangs him on the head with it.

"You want a purse," she says, "try this one." We calm her down and the guy is booked. We find out later, he's been mugging women all over the area.

That case, and scores of others . . . we have to handle them while I'm still investigating the hijacking. I can only give a bit of time to the hijack because there's always something else coming up. But then I get a break. The patrolman who busted up the attempted hijack calls me. This Kinsella, he says he's seen two of the hijackers drinking in Bo's bar, the Tik Tok. Not only that, he has the license plate number of one of the guy's car.

Beautiful. I have the number checked out and find it belongs to a Joseph Hadley in the Bronx. The Identification Section tells me this Hadley is thirty-seven and has a record for gambling. But they don't have any photograph I can use for identification . . . I'm going to have to go round to the address with Kinsella to see if the patrolman can confirm Hadley is the guy we want. Kinsella, Eddie Dillon and me, we go round and there in front of the building is the station wagon with the license plate Kinsella noted.

I tell Kinsella that when he sees this Hadley, he's got to give me a sign to indicate whether or not he's one of the hijackers. Eddie Dillon goes round to the back to make sure Hadley doesn't try to take off while we're at the front.

Hadley's wife answers the door and after I've identified myself, she goes to fetch her husband.

He's a large, solemn-faced guy, with dark brown hair. When Kinsella sees him, he nods at me. This is one of the hijackers. I feel pretty good, but I don't let this Hadley know it.

"Will you come with us to the stationhouse?" I ask him.

"What's this all about?" he wants to know.

"You're a suspect in a hijack-kidnap case," I say, and I go on to advise him of his rights.

Hadley looks shook. "I don't know what you're talking about," he says.

Eddie Dillon comes in and he goes with Hadley into his bedroom while Hadley gets dressed. The wife is in some state . . . almost in tears. We take Hadley to the 41st Precinct and put him in custody. Then Eddie, Kinsella and me, we go to the Tik Tok to see if the other guy Kinsella spotted is there.

Down at the far end of the saloon, there's a man cleaning a table top with a rag. I look at Kinsella and he says, "Yeah, that's the guy." We identify ourselves and the guy says his name is Carl Vincent. I tell him of his rights and ask him to come to the stationhouse. Vincent doesn't say much. He just puts on his jacket and comes out to the car.

In the car, heading back to the 41st Precinct, I tell this Vincent he's been identified as the driver of the car involved in an attempted hijacking.

He seems like a slow thinker . . . there's no reaction except he says, "Oh, no, I didn't do that."

"What d'you mean, you didn't do that?" I come back. "Did you do something?" This Vincent, he doesn't say anything to that.

In the stationhouse, we bring in Vincent and there's Hadley. I watch them both for any reaction between them. But there's nothing that I can see, other than them knowing each other a bit because they both use the same saloon. I decide to take Hadley into the interrogation room.

As I sit there looking at him, I think about the complaint form which gives the descriptions of the three men who tried to take off the beer truck. The first is white, 30, about 5 feet 11 inches, 180 pounds, black wavy hair, dark brown three-quarter coat, with a gun.

The second is white, 25, 5 feet 7 inches, 140 pounds, brown straight hair, dark jacket. The third is white, no age, 5 feet 11 inches, stocky, brown three-quarter coat.

This Hadley fits the first and the third description. In fact, as I'm looking at him, he's wearing a brown three-quarter-length coat. Vincent, outside, fits the description of the second man.

I start questioning Hadley, but he denies everything. He says at the time of the hijack, he was visiting his wife in a hospital, but he admits he can't prove it. I keep on at him, but he won't budge. He insists he's innocent.

It's the same with Vincent when I take him on. He's sweating, but he claims he knows nothing about it. "The hell with it," I say. "I'm booking you." Both Hadley and Vincent are taken to pre-arraignment.

Later, we get hold of the truck driver, Wilson, and show him pictures of Hadley and Vincent, mixed up with other pictures of other guys. He selects Hadley and Vincent as the hijackers.

It looks solid—two witnesses identifying them, one witness a patrolman, the other witness the victim who saw them close-up.

At first I'm pleased with the case, but after a while I find myself thinking more and more about these two, Hadley and Vincent. There's something, particularly about Hadley, with his clean, neat home, his appearance, which doesn't fit in. I begin to get bothered.

There's something else. During one hearing in court, a couple of detectives from Queens come up to me. They claim Hadley is innocent. They say they both know the guy and he just isn't the type. I tell them both Hadley and Vincent have been properly identified. One of these detectives is real insistent, almost threatening.

"Look, Schiano," he says, "you'd better be careful. You could wind up in trouble, making a false arrest. Maybe the chief inspector will get after your ass." I know this is bullshit —everything has been done by the book.

"Don't threaten me," I tell him. "I got a job to do and I'm doing it."

The case against Hadley and Vincent is so strong that even if I think they're innocent, I can't stop them going to trial. All I've got is an instinct that something's wrong. To a detective, a feeling like that is important, but to a court it's nothing. Imagine a detective on the stand telling the judge, "Your honor, my instinct tells me this guy is guilty." Instinct doesn't matter. Facts matter.

The more I think about it, the more I know there's only one way to be sure. I've got to do some more investigating. If Hadley and Vincent are innocent, some other guys are guilty and I've got to find them.

I backtrack to John Stern, the guy who was issued the

vehicle inspection number which I found on the abandoned car.

Didn't it have to be his car that was used? But Stern doesn't fit the descriptions of any of the hijackers. He tells me he sold the auto to a fellow worker at the Calverton Oil Company.

"Who?" I ask.

"Peter Faso," Stern says. And he shows me the receipt. Stern also tells me that Faso had mentioned to him that the car had blown its transmission on the Pelham Parkway . . . and that's where the abandoned Chevy was found.

I go to the Calverton Oil Company where this Faso works as a tractor trailer driver and I pick him up. He fits the description of a couple of the wanted men and, later, Patrolman Kinsella identifies him as the third hijacker.

Now we've got three guys, but that doesn't get Hadley and Vincent off the hook. Like them, Faso denies knowing anything about the beer truck caper. But, with Faso, I find an opening. Someone's lying. Because Faso denies that he bought Stern's car.

I don't tell him that I've got the registration with his signature from Stern. I ask him if he knows Hadley and Vincent. This Faso seems puzzled and he says he's never heard of them. I ask him if he knows the Tik Tok. He says he doesn't.

I put more work in, trying to connect Faso to Hadley and Vincent. I can't find the connection. But I do find out something. I find out that Bo has put up bail for Hadley. That doesn't help Hadley, because my old pal Bo is no angel.

Back to the Tik Tok I go. It crosses my mind that maybe the beer in the hijacked truck was meant for Bo and the Tik Tok.

238

The first thing Bo says is that Hadley and Vincent had no part in the hijack. I ask him why he put up the bail for Hadley.

"I know I shouldn't have done it," he says. "I'm still on parole and I shouldn't do that sort of thing." His explanation is that Hadley's wife came to him for advice about bail for her husband because she knew Bo had done a jail term. Bo explained the procedure to her, but she was too upset to handle it. She begged him to help her out, and finally Bo agreed to stand bail and he got Hadley out.

"The guy's lost his job because of you arresting him," Bo tells me. "He was in trouble and I helped him. If that gets me in trouble, well, that's too bad. I'm telling you, you've got the wrong guys."

I'd heard that song before, but it didn't make me any happier. I still couldn't dig up any connection between Hadley and Faso, or between Vincent and Faso. But I was sure this Faso was guilty. It was that instinct again.

The months slipped by and I had my plate full with other cases. I got permission from my boss, Lieutenant Bill Poster of the 41st Precinct, to keep on at the hijack case when I had a spare minute from chasing the punks who infest the South Bronx. This lieutenant, he knew I was worried we might have the wrong guys, but some of the other cops I work with, they laughed at me and called me a nut for refusing to leave the hijack case alone.

"What's the matter, Tony?" they used to say. "Haven't you got enough work to do?"

They were right. There was more than enough as the summer went by and then the autumn. In the South Bronx, when the weather turns good, people turn bad and you can get blood messing up the streets. One day, there's blood at

239

167th Street and Southern Boulevard. I'm riding in an un-marked car with two other detectives, one of them a guy called Milt Bronson, who's always good for a laugh. We get a message over the radio that shots have been fired on 167th Street.

We're close, so we turn on the siren and whip over there. There's a crowd gathered around a guy who's lying in the gutter and there are other people hiding behind garbage cans and behind the pillars of the El. This guy in the gutter has a bullet hole in his head and that's where the blood is coming from.

Some of the onlookers are shouting and pointing at a small restaurant nearby. "The guy's in there," they yell. "He's got a gun. He just shot Willie." Milt Bronson and me, we head for the restaurant and from the doorway we can see this big guy in a white apron, evidently a cook, standing behind the counter with the gun still in his hand. He points it at us and he shouts, "Stay back!"

I've got a gun in my hand and I could take a shot at him, but there's other people in the restaurant, lying on the floor, and I don't want to take a chance. This cook starts retreating to the back of the restaurant and for a moment he looks away. That's our chance. We rush in and I take a flying swan dive over the counter, landing on him and grabbing his gun. It's a .38. We put the cuffs on him.

When we pull him to his feet, we see he's crying. He tells us that this Willie outside in the gutter had been trying to start an affair with his wife. The wife didn't want any part of him and chased him out. But, later, this Willie returned with five other guys and the cook had to use his gun, he says, to defend himself.

As we're taking him out of the restaurant, the cook asks

us to turn off the light under a big pot of soup. Milt turns off the light and then he takes a little bowl and he scoops up some of the soup. It smells good. We're waltzing out of the restaurant with our prisoner and as we do, here's Milt eating the soup from his container. Well, it's lunchtime and he's hungry. Later, we find out that Willie survived the shooting but he lost an eye.

When you've got cases like that coming up all the time, it's tough to find time for anything else, like the hijack. A year went by and I wasn't getting anywhere. Eighteen months and still nothing.

In September, 1971, twenty months after the hijack, there's a hearing in Supreme Court for Hadley, Vincent and Faso. This is the first time I meet the assistant district attorney who's going to handle the case. His name's Paul London.

Right from the start, we don't get along. It begins when London shows up for a meeting nearly two hours late. The next day, I turn up an hour late. We start yelling at each other. When it's quieted down a bit, I turn over to London all the material I've picked up in the case. I tell this London, I feel we've grabbed the wrong guys, Hadley and Vincent. Faso I'm not worried about.

I suggest the Bronx District Attorney, Burton Roberts, should be told about it, and London agrees. Roberts is a tough, energetic prosecutor and he sends word that I should look deeper into the case. Some people have the wrong idea about DAs. They think all the district attorney wants is convictions. That isn't necessarily true. A good DA isn't interested in convicting innocent people. There's enough guilty ones to go round.

While I'm working with London, I start asking him to quash the charges against Hadley and Vincent. Because now

I'm sure we got the wrong guys. London says he'll have to apply to the court after making up the proper papers.

I got the impression that London is disgusted with the whole case because of the mixed-up identifications. He tells me he's resigning from the DA's office in November to go into private practice.

"Hey," I tell him, "you make sure you get these guys, Hadley and Vincent, out of this mess. I busted two innocent men and I want them cleared." He tells me not to worry. It'll be done.

By the fall of 1971, I've almost finished that extra room on my house which I was telling Eddie Dillon about the night of the hijack. I work on it during holidays and in my spare time. It's a sonofabitch. If I'd known how much work it was going to take, I'd never have started on it. I nearly fry myself, working on the roof during the hottest part of the summer. I call the room The Mausoleum. Now I decide it'll have to wait.

I go to my immediate boss, Lieutenant Poster, and I ask for permission to work on the hijack case in my spare time. A cop can't follow a case out of duty hours unless he has official permission.

Poster . . . he's a tall, sleek-haired guy who joined the department the same time I did and graduated with me. He's a good cop and I can't say any more about any guy than that. He's sharp and he's got that talent you can't learn . . . leadership. You want to do a good job for him. He doesn't have to order you or bear down on you, because you give him 100 per cent without that sort of stuff.

He knows all about the hijack case and how I feel about it. But a request like mine, it's unusual. Most cops consider their job is done when they've gathered the evidence and arrested a suspect.

It's up to the defense to try to prove a suspect is innocent, not the police department. A conscientious detective will tell the DA's office he's uneasy about the guilt of a man he's arrested, but normally he'll leave it at that.

After listening to me, Poster says it's okay for me to work in my own time. "But I want you to remember one thing," the lieutenant says. "This hijack case mustn't interfere with your work during normal duty hours. We've already got too much on our hands."

That's good enough for me. I feel good that the lieutenant doesn't laugh at me, like some of the other cops.

Patrolman Kinsella, even though he identified Hadley and Vincent as the hijackers, he thinks like me by now. He thinks maybe we got the wrong guys. Like me, he gets permission to work on the case in his own time. It's no fun. We chase down false leads, knock on doors, wait for people to come home. And all the time we're questioning people. We meet people who talk too much and we meet people who don't like cops and won't talk at all. Faso won't help and I can't blame him. After all, I locked the guy up. But we come up with the names of two of his pals, Joe Infantino and Bob Gamble, both one-time employees of the Calverton Oil Company, where he worked.

That was part of our trouble—we were assuming the key to the hijack was the Tik Tok. It wasn't. It was the Calverton Oil Company. We find out that it's Gamble who took over the car and the license plate of the dead guy, Hinch. Also, this Joe Infantino fits the description of one of the hijackers.

I notice that there's a similarity between the one couple, Faso and Infantino, and the other couple, Hadley and Vincent.

At the end of September, 1971, I arrest Infantino and book him at the 41st Precinct. I try to talk to him as I fill in the

243

arrest papers, but he won't say anything. I tell him I'll try to get him a lighter sentence if he'll give up his accomplices. Nothing.

"I don't know what you're talking about," he keeps saying.

I'm swearing to myself at all the paperwork involved in an arrest when this Infantino suddenly says, "Hey, officer, I want to talk to you." Wow! Now I feel good. The guy's going to come clean.

"Talk," I tell him.

"No, I don't want to talk here," Infantino says. I know what he means. When a suspect decides to inform, he wants to do it in private.

Patrolman Kinsella is there as well, so the three of us head for the interview rooms, but both are occupied. We have to settle for the detectives' lavatory.

I'm half sitting on a washbasin. Kinsella, holding a notebook, is near the urinals. Infantino is leaning against a radiator.

"Okay," I say, "what d'you want to tell us?"

"Let's make a deal," Infantino says.

"What?" I say. "What kind of deal?"

"Money," Infantino says. I can feel the anger coming up inside. "How much?" I say.

"I'll give you $2,500 to drop the case against me now," Infantino says. "I don't want to be bothered with it. Get me off the hook."

I stand up and start towards Infantino. Kinsella is already moving. I'm just about to throw a punch when the patrolman grabs me around the arms and holds me.

"Take it easy, Tony," he says. I'm still trying to get at Infantino. "You scumbag bastard," I shout. "You think you

244

can buy me, you rat bastard. Well, I'll tell you something
. . . now I'm charging you with bribery as well." And we
book him for that.

It all starts coming in a rush. I go after Bob Gamble and
I find him at an address in Far Rockaway. I arrest him, and
Kinsella identifies him as one of the three hijackers. Now, at
last, Hadley and Vincent can be dismissed from the case. I
go to see London and he agrees to make the formal application to the court.

The morning of November 10, 1971, I walk into Bronx
Supreme Court. Hadley and Vincent are standing with their
attorneys in front of the bench, waiting for the judge. Behind
them, in the public seats, I can see Mrs. Hadley and her
children.

I slip into a seat next to her and I say, very quietly, "Mrs.
Hadley, I have a surprise for you . . . I think your husband
is going to walk out of here today a free man."

Mrs. Hadley, she's a nice plump housewife type . . . she
gives a little gasp and her face lights up. The judge comes in
and London gets up.

"Your honor," he says, "I would like to make application
to dismiss the two defendants, Hadley and Vincent, on their
own recognizance. The People now believe there is reason-
able doubt about the guilt of these two men and therefore we
ask for their dismissal from the case."

The judge grants the application. Hadley's shoulders sag
and he slumps down in his chair, shaking his head as if he
can't believe it. Vincent, he's a slow thinker and he stares
around as if he's trying to make out what's happened. Mrs.
Hadley is clutching my arm so hard I can feel her nails
through the cloth.

When it's all over, Hadley comes up to me outside the

courtroom. I can see traces of tears on that solemn mug of his.

"Thank God somebody believed me," he says. He knows how close he came to a jail sentence, I guess. London told me later that without the deeper investigation, there was no reason to believe Hadley and Vincent wouldn't have been convicted by any jury.

A reporter on the *Daily News,* Eddie Kirkman, picks up the story which runs under the headline "Cop Clears Two He Had Grabbed."

It's followed up by other reporters, and a TV crew sets up an interview with Hadley. He's had a bad time, losing his job and worrying about the charge for nearly two years. He can't forget that.

Talking about the case in front of the cameras, he says, "It's great. But why did Schiano take so long to prove me innocent?"

What the hell . . . cops who come on the job expecting thanks from the public soon learn better.

Later, I drop in on the Tik Tok and there's Bo leaning against the bar. "I knew all the time those guys didn't do it," he says. "They ain't the type for a job like that."

It had to happen. In September, 1972, Vincent sues me for false arrest. The case is still pending.

I'm still a serving police officer. A member of the New York Police Department. The department makes a good target and there are people who like nothing better than to take aim at it.

But I'm grateful to the department because, without it I could have ended up badly. A punk. Or in a job where the only excitement is picking up the pay packet at the end of the week.

My father came to this country with nothing but his honesty. All his life, he knew what it was to be poor and he didn't find any fun in that. He wanted me to do better than he did and, I guess I have. It's the same with me. I want my kids to go further than me.

I've been lucky. I know it. A few inches . . . that's all it would have taken for the knives, the guns, to have finished me. The knives and the guns and the men who use them, they're still out there, and as a police officer I'll go among them until the day I sign my official retirement papers.

Or until a guy with a knife or a gun comes at me from the shadows and there's no luck left.

chestful of medals for his exploits. Go with him into the "houses of horror," as he runs the gauntlet of muggers who line the halls, and finally makes an incriminating buy from the pusher who extracts the heroin packets from the dainty panties he wears. Go with Solo as he brazens his way through a confrontation with suspicious sellers who insist on watching him take a fix—as he chases a suspect down a collapsing staircase or puzzles out the selling gimmick of a bogus "balloon man."

SOLO reads like an imaginary adventure tale, with bizarre characters, bloody encounters and narrow escapes—but every word is true. This is the junkies' world. "Not even the cops know what it is like," says Tony Solo, "except for the few guys like me who go underground. It's cancerous. And I have to become a part of the scene."